WELCOME TO THE COUNTRY

Things You Need to Know When Moving to Rural Virginia

by Frank Levering

BALLYSHANNON FUND

WWW.BALLYSHANNONFUND.COM

Welcome to the Country: Things you Need to Know when Moving to Rural Vurginia
by Frank Levering

The Ballyshannon Fund of the
Charlottesville Area Community Foundation
1801 Bundoran Drive
Charlottesville, VA 22959
www.ballyshannonfund.com

First Printing: October 2008
Printed in Lynchburg, Virginia
Designed by Keith Damiani, Sequoia Design
Cover photo © 2005 by Robert Llewellyn

ISBN 978-0-615-22842-6

CONTENTS

*You can find links to many of the organizations mentioned in this book,
along with other helpful resources about rural Virginia, at*

www.BallyshannonFund.com

WELCOME

Welcome to the country. Good to see you here.

Now imagine, for a moment, that you've just knocked on the door of a house in the Virginia countryside. The sun's going down, and though the slanting light is rosy and mellow across the rolling fields and forests, you're a little nervous. After all, maybe you've just moved here, or are getting ready to move. In either case, your life is changing. You've left a city or a suburb behind, and now—of all things!—you've thump-thumped off the road with a flat tire, and you're standing on the porch of a complete stranger's house hoping for a little help. Certainly, you're anxious about your flat...But truth be told, you're here for more than help. Deeper down, you're feeling a bit like a fish out of water, and you're hoping to forge your first connection with a native of this valley. You're hoping that person knows how to make a newcomer feel welcome.

Now imagine that the person who says "Hello" has a friendly face. You explain why you're here, and apologize for the imposition.

What you didn't expect is that this native who enters the house and returns with a compressed air bottle doesn't appear to think you're imposing. "Glad to help." But despite the friendliness, there's an awkwardness you're still feeling. You sense that this stranger would like to ask some questions. After all, you're moving in just across the ridge there. You're a new neighbor, and this native has reason to get to know you. What you do with your newly acquired property—and the perspective you have on the values of other rural property-owners—will inevitably affect the lives of your neighbors. Thanking your new neighbor, you promise to return the air bottle as soon as you inflate the tire, and walk back to your car.

The air bottle does the trick. Breathing easier, on the walk back to the porch you notice the hay bales strewn across the fields; there's a very large tractor with a big cab parked just on the other side of a fence; and all of a sudden it dawns on you that the person you're talking to is a *bona fide* farmer.

A farmer. This is the sort of creature you've read about in the newspaper or seen interviewed on the TV news. You've never had occasion to get to know one, and now this stranger who steps back onto the porch has proved to be the very soul you needed in an emergency. You've made your money in an urban profession, and here is this person who somehow earns a living and does something—not entirely clear what—with that oversized tractor. Bales hay, maybe?

> What you do with your newly acquired property—and the perspective you have on the values of other rural property-owners—will inevitably affect the lives of your neighbors.

You figure it probably has something to do with hay. Not wanting to be seen as a greenhorn, or seem nosey, you leave your questions in your throat. Next time.

"Thank you, again," you say.

"Any time! Just glad to help!"

Funny thing, you think to yourself, driving down the road. You had questions—and this native, you sensed, had questions. Yet neither one of you asked a single one. An opportunity lost, you're thinking to yourself—to bridge that awkward gap.

But there was one good thing: That farmer was friendly. No. Two good things: That farmer was friendly *and* eager to help.

Although this is a fictional scene, the fact is there are many rural Virginians who would answer to this description. But, in some cases, it's true that friendliness doesn't always come so easily. Rural Virginia is beset by some daunting challenges—skyrocketing land prices, infrastructure and school deficiencies, rising property taxes and the loss of youth to urban areas. Rural residents trying to earn a living and accommodate the pace of change feel the strain of those challenges. Strains and pressures can make some folks very cautious.

In this guidebook, we aim to offer you the same kind of help and friendliness as our farmer. So, *Welcome to the country. We're glad you're here!* We want to know what your hopes are in living here. We hope you'll stay.

That said, we certainly don't mean to exclude natives from the ranks of our readers. For natives, too, can add to their store of knowledge by reading this book. So, to those hardy souls long established down a Virginia lane, you come along, too! We're getting ready to follow a road deep into the heart of rural Virginia.

We really want to explore this place with you. We aim to introduce you to the way things are done here, who does them, and why—they've been doing it a long time, and chances are, they know what they're doing. We're here to teach and to learn, to get better acquainted, and come away better informed—and maybe even a little wiser!

ROAD MAP
TO
RURAL
VIRGINIA

By the time you finish reading *Welcome to the Country* you'll know, likely, a fair bit more than you do now about the cultural traditions, unwritten codes of behavior, laws, and farming practices in rural Virginia—with particular attention to the ten-county Central Virginia heartland that straddles the Blue Ridge Mountains. This region of often exponential growth is comprised of Albemarle, Nelson, Louisa, Orange, Fluvanna, Madison, Greene, Augusta, Rockingham, and Rockbridge counties. If you're a newcomer to this ten-county region—or, indeed, to any predominantly rural region in Virginia—this book will help you adapt to your surroundings and live harmoniously with your neighbors. If you're a native, reading this book will offer you a crisper understanding of and more up-to-date information about the place you have long called home.

Consider this book a cultural road map to life along some of Virginia's most intriguing back roads. It's a guide to the established customs of the countryside: what people do to earn a living here; how people who own property get along with others; and why farmers and farmland must never become marginalized. Our primary goal is simple: to promote mutual respect and enhanced communication between newcomers and natives. We think that mutual respect and more open lines of communication are made possible by opportunities to learn and to expand our vision. With lessons drawn from numerous interviews, extensive travel in Virginia, and our own combined experience as members of a rural culture, we hope that *Welcome to the Country* will provide such an opportunity.

We believe that—working alongside one another—those who are new to rural Virginia and those who have been here a long while can share a community and landscape—and together achieve great things.

I
n central Virginia, as well as some other parts of the state, the past few decades have witnessed an extraordinary urban-to-rural migration. The splendor of the countryside, the yearning to escape the urban fast lane, and the lure of a simpler life lived closer to nature have all combined to bring flocks of "metropolitans"—folks accustomed to the brisk rhythms and vibrant cultural activities of cities—to rural areas. Most of these areas, including the central Virginia heartland, have traditionally been farming communities, the sorts of places where Farm Bureau baseball caps shade the eyes of tractor-drivers, where a crossroads store is a haven for dusty pickup trucks, where cows—and crops—and the weather—are hotter topics than the latest misadventures of Hollywood celebrities in *People* magazine.

With this major in-migration has come the clamor of saws and hammers, as new houses go up and lawn grass is sewn where once was a rolling pasture. With it, too, have come jobs, greener pastures for local economies, and a more robust bottom line for any business fortunate enough to service the needs and tastes of the urban transplants. It has also brought in some newcomers who value the work and the wisdom of farmers, and who have a keen interest in preserving the agrarian heritage of Virginia's rural areas.

But along with these and other positives have come additional strains on county services, as local governments weigh the *pros* of a pumped-up tax base with the *cons* of "progress" that threatens to reshape the character of rural communities. Along with the positives, too, has often come a dearth of knowledge and understanding about the agrarian way of life—a cultural "tone deafness"—leading frequently to conflict between transplants and natives.

One of the natives we interviewed expressed his perspective on the conflict this way: **"People moving into rural areas like the idea of farms. They just don't understand farming."**

A recent arrival from the Washington area expressed a newcomer's perspective very differently: "People out here, they're not very trusting when people move in, are they? Seems like they'll just sort of keep an eye on everything you're doing. And not tell you much."

Another native expressed the friction this

CULTURES

way: "There's a widely divergent economic base between newcomers—who often have higher incomes—and locals, who may have less income. Newcomers don't want industry and they know how to work the system to prevent anything that threatens their land. They want to "protect" what they've purchased. This isn't always good for natives, especially younger ones, who might ask: 'Protect from what?' With no jobs, natives cannot afford a house."

Martha Walker, Ph.D., a Community Viability Specialist with Virginia Cooperative Extension, summarized the state of affairs this way, in a *Roanoke Times* article entitled *The Reality of Rural Life:* "Each side wants to be engaged with each other, but they choose different paths to do so, and they don't take the time to talk to each other first."

This culture clash—this friction point where two world views rub against each other—takes many forms. Picture this scene: on a sinuous country road a tractor trundles along, its driver getting the workday started by taking the highway to a distant field. Behind the tractor with its wide farm implement attached, a new resident of the area follows impatiently in a BMW, unable to pass because of the road's incessant curves. Finally, his patience frayed to the snapping point, the BMW driver lays on his horn in frustration, a prolonged blast which the farmer interprets as "Pull off the damn road and get out of my way!"

With a wide machine and nowhere to pull over, the farmer doesn't budge. "Who owns this highway, anyway?" he probably thinks. He's paid his taxes same as the car driver—and he'll be damned if he's pulling off into the ditch to accommodate the speed-lust of one of "them."

This scene isn't fictional. It's one of the many farm-equipment-on-the-highway incidents reported by farmers we've talked to. Nor is the following scene fictional: A new resident of a rural community crosses paths with a farmer at a country store. It's lunch hour, and as rural folks often do, the farm-er is eating his lunch and drinking his Pepsi on a bench outside the store. "What was that

stuff you were spraying with this morning?" the new resident asks the farmer, a neighbor on one side of the new resident's property.

The farmer's neck stiffens, as he recalls the many times he's been told by some new "expert" what he can and can't do on his own land. "Why do you ask?"

The new resident tries to smile—he'd thought his tone was pleasant enough, he certainly hadn't meant to offend. And besides, doesn't he have a right to know? The wind was up a little that morning, and whatever the farmer was spraying could have drifted over onto his property. "Well," he says, not quite daring to bring up that point, "I was just curious."

The farmer smiles but replies without warmth "It's nothing for you to worry about." With a nod, he touches his cap and returns to his lunch.

These two scenes—both slices from real life—dramatize a fault line in rural Virginia: the tension between the traditional prerogatives of farmers in going about their business, in making their work pay off, and the imported cultural norms of newcomers, norms that may view an impediment on the highway or a pesticide wafting airborne as non-negotiable detriments to life in the country. In each case, communication, such as it was, degenerated quickly into open hostility. In each case, the prospect for further communication and eventual mutual understanding was aborted at the outset, with opinions freezing solid, unlikely ever to thaw.

It doesn't have to be that way. Folks moving to rural Virginia can offer an infusion of much-needed energy, resources, and a willingness to make a positive difference in their adopted communities. Natives can bring to the table tried-and-true practices and wisdom, and a long-standing commitment to sound land management and neighborly cooperation.

. . . .

Working together, newcomers and natives have the opportunity to make rural Virginia an even better place to live, creating together a new patchwork quilt that blends the wisdom of experience with fresh ideas and perspectives.

. . . .

By welcoming differing views, a community creates a chance for the best and most workable ideas to win out. By keeping our minds wide open, a rural community can know and value itself, achieve greater capacity, enrich its culture, and diversify its perspective.

MAKING THE MOVE

Perhaps it's inevitable, our popular culture being what it is, that more often than not, a city-dweller's notions about country life are more than a little idealized. Despite some negative media depictions and stereotypes, TV shows like *Green Acres* and *The Waltons*, magazines like *Country Living* and *Blue Ridge Country*, advertisements that depict motorists driving blissfully down pastoral highways, have all implanted generally idyllic images in urban minds. Out in the countryside, it's easy to imagine, it's all about beauty, tranquility, open space, a slower pace — a simpler life. Gone is the grinding urban commute, the frenetic crowds at the mall. Gone is the smoggy sky and the background hum of freeway traffic within earshot. Out in the country the birds sing sweetly, and even the breeze smells sweet. Out in the country, life is natural, unencumbered, free of nuisance.

Too often, this "Humpty-Dumpty" of romanticized imagery takes a hard fall. What a newcomer discovers after settling in to country life can often come as a shock: malodorous farm practices, where the occasional unfamiliar smells almost stick to your skin; abrasive noises that puncture peace and quiet at early and late hours; snail-paced farm equipment like the tractor that incensed our BMW driver; harvested forests that to an untrained urban eye may resemble the aftermath of Sherman's March; the sport of hunting with — horrors! — guns! Right there in the pickup cab's rear window! ...and along with those guns, dead animals being dragged around by rough-looking characters in camouflage outfits — and rifle and shotgun blasts that seem to come out of nowhere, scorching the air, making an urban skin crawl, causing parents to sheepdog their kids to the safety of the house. As Linda Hogan, who moved with her husband Doug to Rockbridge County from the New York City suburbs, told the *Roanoke Times:* "People hunt here, so you hear rifles going off. We weren't used to that before."

Like the Hogans before they moved, eighty percent of Americans live in major metropolitan areas, those urban concentric rings where the major airlines fly, where metroplex theaters and gridlock traffic reign supreme. For the increasing percentage that moves far from the madding crowds of urban existence, it can be as strange as Mars out in the countryside. A planet apart from where they used to live — and a far cry, very likely, from their expectations.

Once newcomers confront the facts of country life, a good many of the agricultural and rural customs and ways of conducting business will strike them as threats to the quality of their new lives. Convenience? A tractor crawling down a public highway is the bane of convenience. Guns blasting away and farm equipment rumbling at six in the morning? Didn't we leave the city to get away from mind-jarring noise?

By the same token, transplants may not be aware that rural communities may not take kindly to glaring, city-style lights obscuring the sky at night; new houses that perch on ridge tops that were formerly pristine natural features; gated property and "No Trespassing" signs that seem to scream: "You may be my neighbor, but I want nothing to do with you." Even seemingly small things — such as not returning a farmer's wave on a country road; not showing any interest in things that are vital to farmers (the weather, the spike in gasoline prices, the rising cost of fertilizer) can brand newcomers as arrogant; as unapproachable "outsiders."

That word "newcomers," by the way. What to make of it? It's such an awkward word that we regret the need to use it. "Transplant" is no better—sounds like a verb, not a noun, something you do with a tree

Wherever folks move into rural areas and small towns in this great country of ours, there's often the risk that things can go the wrong way: They may be "newcomers" for forty years! Minimum. This doesn't always happen—that's an urban myth, fueled occasionally (and understandably) by just a tad of cultural paranoia.

But, yes, it is true that sometimes, in some clannish places perhaps embittered by job losses or poverty rates—and still resistant to change—newcomers can never quite shed the skin of where they came from. No matter how hard they pitch in to help their new community. No matter how well their son plays high school football or their daughter plays her roles at the community theater. Newcomers—"She's not from here"—as opposed to those whose families have lived here for generations, can be a native's reflexive reduction of a woman who's lived and participated in her adopted community for all of thirty years.

In hardcore cases like these—honestly, what are you gonna do? It's human nature to categorize someone as not belonging to our tribe. The reality, though, is that rural places are anything but monolithic. In rural Virginia, it's increasingly rare to find a community so isolated, so hostile to change, that newcomers can never be accepted. That's a scriptwriter's broad-brushed conception of rural life—a fiction penned by one who's never spent time in rural culture. "Dust pictures" is the inside-Hollywood slang for films of this sort—telling stories that take place down "dusty" roads. (Or worse, down wild rivers. The film Deliverance, *for example, was a portrayal that left an indelible—not to mention harshly unfair and inaccurate—impression of Southern mountain people.)*

you just bought down at the nursery. The problem, literally, is this: Try as we might, we can't find a word in the English language that suffices quite as well. "Outsider?" Clearly, that loaded, prejudicial word just won't do!

There are compelling reasons for "newcomers" or "transplants" (for lack of better words) to acknowledge the centrality of farming in a rural culture and the vital role it plays in supporting the local, regional, national, and perhaps even international community and economy. The reasons? Nope—not because farmers "were here first."

For starters, learning about agriculture, forestry and the people who do it is one of the better ways to win over the hearts of rural people. There's nothing quite as appealing as paying keen attention to, and acknowledging, what another human being has to do to ensure that his children are clothed, fed, and get a good education. Another reason, as one farmer stated bluntly: "Eating is not an option." The bottom line—no matter how much money you may have raked in back in the city—is that farmers put food on your table. They do that. How basic—how crucial—is that?

Farmers are proud of their ability to do that—the acquired skill and the sheer nerve it takes—always at the mercy of the weather, commodity prices, and competition from abroad. Chances are, you're no wizard at producing food yourself—few Americans are. Even if you're a decent backyard tomato-grower, do you have what it takes to reliably, consistently produce food for thousands of consumers?

Learning more about how American agriculture ensures the quality of your life—where food "is not an option"—is a civics lesson on a par with taking the time to know the issues in an election. Ultimately, taking the time to learn about farming will reward you in the form of no unpleasant surprises. It will help build trust, cooperation, and a sense of having mutual membership and stake in your new community.

But before we dig deeper into agriculture, let's take a panoramic look around us. And let's go back in time. Few places in America — if any — can rival Virginia in the wealth of its landscapes and the sweep of its past.

VIRGINIA'S *unrivaled* HEARTLAND

Let your eyes drift across the official state travel map of Virginia, the kind of map you pick up at a state-line Welcome Center, and you'll see many things. You'll see the names of cities and towns and hamlets. You'll see the blue and red and gray squiggles of highways. You'll see where rail lines go, and where you can land your airplane. You'll see shades of green denoting mountains and parks. You'll see the meandering course of rivers, seemingly quixotic at times, and the blue amoebas of lakes.

Then there are the names of counties. Each name with a flavor, a mystique. In the central Virginia heartland that lies at the epicenter of urban in-migration you'll see the names straddling the forest green of the Washington National Forest and Shenandoah National Park. Albemarle. Augusta. Fluvanna…names that sparked the name of an apple variety in great demand in Queen Victoria's court (the Albemarle Pippin). Names inspired by what Thomas Jefferson regarded as one of nature's sublimest works (Rockbridge County, named for Natural Bridge).

Virginia's official map doesn't tell the stories of these counties. It leaves that to historians, to journalists, to the people who live there themselves. These are continuing stories, and each county has its own to tell—tales unique to that place and how it evolved. Rockbridge County knew the likes of Robert E. Lee and Stonewall Jackson, legends in wartime, cast also in roles (college president and professor, respectively) that aren't the first things that come to mind. Orange County was home to the man Jefferson called the greatest of his generation — our Constitution's guiding light, James Madison. Nelson County inspired stories that shaped enduring national perceptions about life in the Blue Ridge and the Great Depression, stories beamed electronically by Schuyler [*pronounced "SKY-LUR"*] native Earl Hamner, Jr., the gentlemanly creator of *The Waltons*. Named for Revolutionary War stalwart Nathanial Greene, Greene County's 20th Century history intertwines with the creation of Shenandoah National Park, a favorite weekend retreat for residents of our nation's Capital.

There's so much more you can say about Virginia's central heartland, if you're receptive to the complexity of an American place. You can talk about the rivers that run through this magnificent country—nothing mighty, on the order of the Mississippi or the Ohio, but rivers like the James, the Shenandoah, and the Rivanna, modestly draining the ancient backbone of the Blue Ridge; and lesser rivers flowing out of the west, rising, in part, from the Shenandoah Mountains.

You can talk about topography—how, from a low-flying plane, the softly Rubens-esque peaks of the Blue Ridge divide the visible world into two halves. First is the Virginia Piedmont—Jefferson's, Madison's, and James Monroe's country—sloping eastward at the foot of the range, rolling, sheltered by the wall of mountains, prodigal in the form of vineyards, orchards, with cultural oases like Charlottesville, an international Mecca. The other half—the Great Valley, one of the garden spots on Earth, once a "breadbasket" in an emerging nation's Civil War—is now a real estate agent's paradise of panoramic views and purple mountains—on both sides.

You can talk about the people who settled this land of gently sculpted earth: Scots-Irish, English, the potpourri of immigrants from far corners of the globe, many of them strangers (when they arrived) to the dense history of ground haunted by the Revolutionary and Civil Wars.

These new Americans brought fresh entrepreneurial energy, new cultural blood, and dreams that could be unleashed in the cradle of American democracy. Across these landscapes, people from an improbably broad spectrum of backgrounds have settled and staked their claims and made the landscape their own: farmed it, developed it, made a small town or even a mid-size city out of it. This central Virginia region we experience today—like the story of the recent urban immigration—is the sum of human yearning for something better. People came, and in varying degrees added to the mix of the way things are. Their assimilation is the construction of America, in microcosm.

Though each history, each experience, is locally specific; though each county boasts its own singular narrative of settlement and topography, a unifying thread throughout this ten-county region is the long shadow of history itself. Perhaps nowhere else in America—and surely nowhere else in the South—has the turbulence of history triggered such a succession of storms; have the words "upheaval," "defeat," "courage," "resilience" had greater resonance. The Colonial period's thirst for independence, and the Revolutionary War that quenched it...the War of 1812, and the trough of depression in agriculture that followed...the cauldron of slavery, and the rise and fall of Virginia's fortunes in the Civil War...World War I and its shattered aftermath, with visionary idealist and Staunton native Woodrow Wilson hip-deep in the search to find enduring peace...the struggle for racial integration, with central Virginia a less-heralded but nonetheless consequential participant. Taken together, these and other headlines from the past have left an indelible legacy, as history has beaten a well-worn path through the hearts and memories of the people who lived here.

It is that sense of history—a deeply-engrained awareness that monumental events have periodically engulfed everything near and dear, putting one's family to the test or snuffing out the lives of ancestors or siblings—that runs like a river through central Virginia. History is etched in the lined faces of older residents—not just the history of social upheaval on a grand scale, but the history of family soil, of droughts like that of the summer of 1988 and of deadly floods like the apocalyptic torrents unleashed by Hurricane Camille in Nelson County.

Throughout it all—just as rugged West Virginia has been stamped by mining, west Texas by cattle ranching, and much of Florida by its sun-drenched coastlines—the rolling topography of central Virginia has traditionally been a haven for agriculture; Virginia's diverse and fertile soils, temperate climate, ample annual rainfall of forty inches or more, and long growing season ensure that. One example: Just west of the Blue Ridge, near Steeles Tavern, Cyrus McCormick's farm was the testing ground for his 1834 invention of the reaping machine. This giant leap for American productivity was accomplished by McCormick at the ripe old age of twenty-five.

Was necessity the mother of invention? The revolution that followed in agriculture may supply the answer, but McCormick, in a sense, was heir to the agrarian incarnation of Thomas Jefferson, a polymath extraordinaire who lived just slightly northeast of McCormick, on the blueblood side of the Blue Ridge.

It is Jefferson, of course, to whom the term "Renaissance man" best applies—to any American, even to this day. But Jefferson the farmer—a tinkerer, like McCormick—in large degree typified the central Virginia landed gentry of his time. As the longing for independence simmered in Colonial Virginia, Jefferson—and other gentlemen of his class like James Madison and John Page—learned how to cook the fledgling dish of democracy, first serving as apprentice chefs in the Virginia House of Burgesses beginning in their mid-twenties. Living year-round on their plantations, these farmer-plutocrats took their responsibility to govern seriously. In the words of Dumas Malone, the Pulitzer Prize-winning University of Virginia historian, for these and many other prominent farmers, "If the country needed you to serve, you had no right to decline."

Because of Jefferson's writings—the voluminous *The Garden and Farm Notebooks*, and the more renowned *Notes on Virginia*—we think of the author of our landmark Declaration of Independence as a champion of farmers. In *Notes on Virginia* appears the famous tribute, "Those who labor in the earth are the chosen people of God," and Jefferson's vision for the new nation he helped create was a patchwork of small farmers.

That vision was influenced by his readings of Virgil and other Roman writers. Jefferson shared Virgil's affection for industrious, virtuous, and independent farmers, responsible citizens who had a stake in the land. Farmers were independent on their own land, Jefferson believed—unlike city-dwellers, who were dependent on others. The "agricultural interest," he wrote, was the soul of the young nation.

In 1782, in his book *Thoughts of an American Farmer on Various Rural Subjects,* Jefferson's contemporary, the French-born J. Hector St. John de Crevecoeur, observed: "The philosopher's stone of an American farmer is to do everything within his own family, to trouble his neighbors by borrowing... as little as possible, and to abstain from buying European commodities. He that follows that golden rule and has a good wife is almost sure of succeeding."

Leaving aside that question of the "good wife," it's apparent that optimism was in the air about farming. Indeed, for Jefferson, the sentiments transcended optimism—farming was nothing short of a noble calling. But on his own nearly 5,000 acre plantation in Albemarle County, Jefferson suffered the slings and arrows of the real world of agricultural economics. Much of Monticello having been inherited from his father, the vast plantation surrounding the celebrated house on the hill was, under much of Jefferson's watch, an unprofitable economic enterprise. Ultimately, though, the larger picture of Jefferson's efforts is more revealing of the man than the cold figures on that bottom line.

For years, as the Colonials won their independence and formed a new nation, the plantation grew tobacco, which was sold to a British merchant. In the mid-1790's, for three unfettered years, Jefferson broke free from the constraints of public service and redirected his plantation away from the tobacco he regarded as a curse. He replaced the soil-depleting plant with wheat and other grains, and became a hands-on farmer—taking meticulous measurements of crop yields, rotating his crops, introducing labor-saving machinery and new breeds of livestock, planting legumes like red clover to improve the soil. This was Jefferson, the focused farmer.

Not that he was following the ploughs. That was a task for slaves, a population ranging from one hundred to one hundred and forty at Monticello, who implemented Jefferson's directives. What Jefferson was doing was throwing himself into the grand scheme of the enterprise, calling himself—perhaps accurately—"the most ardent farmer in Virginia."

In *The Garden and Farm Notebooks*, Jefferson chronicles his many years of agricultural experiments, some of them conducted in his 1,000-foot-long vegetable garden. Here one glimpses the famously inquisitive mind, as Jefferson wants to know what fruits and vegetables and new breeds of livestock will do best under Monticello's conditions, whether olive varieties from Italy can be grown in Albemarle County. Over his lifetime—as but one example—Jefferson experimented with thirty-seven varieties of peaches. Working with an overseer, his results were often impressive: Jefferson's fruits and vegetables garnered accolades from friends who sampled them at his dining table. His cherries he deemed fit for after-dinner picking (and eating) with his grandchildren, and Jefferson's favorite vegetable—English peas—thrived under his husbandry.

For all that, the mellifluous word "Monticello" might well have been penned by the estate's proprietor in crimson ink. Lucia Stanton, the Shannon Senior Historian at Monticello, believes the plantation never turned a profit. "Jefferson," she told us, "was always writing letters to people he owed money to, saying, 'Well, it was a short crop this year,' or 'We couldn't get the flour down to Richmond.' Just constantly explaining why he wasn't making a certain payment. He was scrambling all his life as a plantation owner."

Periodically, tobacco returned, like an unwanted stepchild, to Monticello: Jefferson was unable to resist the lure of a potentially profitable crop. Still, the plantation swam in red ink. Early on, Jefferson abandoned the elementary exercise of adding up what he'd spent and comparing that figure with what he'd taken in. Perhaps it was too torturous, too painful to contemplate. When Jefferson stepped down as President in 1809—from a presidency that had seen far more momentous events than the fate of his plantation—he turned much of the farming operation over to his grandson, and focused on the industries of the plantation: the mills, the textile manufacturing, the nail-making factory.

The rest is sadness. Jefferson's zeal, his ardent reformations in the 1790's, left him mired in financial failure. Even his one true invention—his improvement on that curved part of the plough that turns the soil, called "the moldboard of least resistance"—was providing scanty financial reward. A former President—the author of an immortal document that has stirred millions—the visionary architect of a mighty nation through the Louisiana Purchase and the explorations of Lewis and Clark (both residents of central Virginia)—had come home from a successful public life to the specter of private failure. At his death on July 4th, 1826, Jefferson's beloved Monticello was some $100,000 in debt, a staggering sum in that early year in our nation's history. Something had gone hauntingly—perhaps inexplicably—wrong.

the Tradition Continues

W
e tell this story at length for several reasons. Jefferson casts a giant's shadow— in central Virginia; our "Mr. Jefferson" remains a towering figure, an international icon drawing visitors to Albemarle County from around the world. To many of the world's greatest statesmen and scholars, Jefferson continues to embody—perhaps alone with Washington and Lincoln—all that is best in the democratic ideal that shaped America and then much of the world.

· ·

But far less attention has centered on the man who farmed, and wrote assiduously about farming. Yet that, too, is Jefferson, and it's a significant part of his legacy not only in the region where he lived, but in how Americans tend even now to think about the practice of farming.

· ·

As a farmer, Jefferson not only articulated the critical societal value of that profession; he also set the standard for his day of meticulous observation and record-keeping. A champion of Enlightenment rationalism, Jefferson practiced his somewhat idiosyncratic version of the scientific method, and gave students and teachers of agriculture a working model for how and why to monitor practices and results. In a sense, Monticello served as laboratory, a kind of privately-financed, proto-Virginia Tech agricultural experiment station. More than Jefferson longed to turn a profit, he yearned to discover what works, and to pass on what he learned.

On the underside of that golden coin—and perhaps of equal value—is the cautionary tale of struggle and debt. Anyone wanting to understand the Farm Crisis that raced like a prairie fire through the Midwest in the 1980s, or the latter-day agonies of tobacco and apple farmers in the South and East as government pressure and distant competition menace the future of farming-as-usual, will read in Jefferson's plantation a larger lesson of farming. They will see how enterprise—and good old American optimism—can be humbled. They will see—in a drought, or during torrential August rains like those of 1795 which devastated Jefferson's corn crop and permanently damaged his soil—how farmers always stand on the front lines of nature's whims. They will see that even a great mind and a devoted student such as Jefferson can stumble in the tenuous venture that is agriculture.

Perhaps it can be summed up this way: Although those "who labor in the earth" may indeed be "the chosen people of God," as Jefferson would have us believe—a bold corrective to a central thesis of the Old Testament!—they also farm at the pleasure of that same fierce God. Theology aside, the hard lessons of their trade cut deep in farmers. Unless you leave the farm—and even that is a dubious proposition—there is no escape from those lessons, short of the psychological phenomenon of denial.

Farmers uniquely absorb the blows that nature and markets and government policy dole out to them, and like good soldiers, try to stand firm. Theirs is a swirling world, more dynamic than the typical non-farmer realizes. The farmers' world is not one of "watching the grass grow" (the proverbial put-down of the rural lifestyle) but is a world of rapid change and urgent problems winging at them like arrows at Little Big Horn. Farming has always been a high-stakes game that may be lost with one errant decision. Across this central Virginia region—and in every farming region in Virginia—Jefferson's heirs, "those who labor in the earth," continue to play that game, and generally play it well. Though this region has evolved quite differently from Jefferson's vision for the nation—a land quilted with small farms—there remain in every direction constellations of farms, interrupted here and there by developments, non-agricultural businesses and towns.

> ◇◇◇◇◇◇◇◇◇◇◇◇◇◇◇◇◇◇◇◇
>
> **The bigger picture is that farming lives on here, adapting to changing conditions, making "new" history every day, each farm a link on an unbroken chain connecting deep into our past.**
>
> ◇◇◇◇◇◇◇◇◇◇◇◇◇◇◇◇◇◇◇◇

There is financial success here—of the sort that eluded Jefferson—in a variety of flagship enterprises: the orchards of Henry Chiles, a ripe kingdom of apples, peaches, and cherries, on a scale perhaps unrivaled in Virginia; beef cattle operations like those managed by veteran stockmen Fred Scott and Corky Shackleford, more recently by a young dynamo named Carl Tinder—ventures that have been models of land stewardship, community involvement, and financial sustainability; and new sorts of farms that are prototypes of adaptive ingenuity—like Steve Murray's marvelously self-designed compost operation, paired with the rental of running trails in his pastures for Charlottesville-area schools and Atlantic Coast Conference teams.

These are but to name a few. The bigger picture is that farming lives on here, adapting to changing conditions, making "new" history every day, each farm a link on an unbroken chain connecting deep into our past. Farmers like those above connect to that distant past, and are the faces of farming today. Their land and their ventures are living history of the sort that schoolchildren—and newcomers—would see and experience, were the world ideal, and learning could always take place on site.

Corky Shackleford's farm is illustrative. On a winter's day after a recent snow, it unfolds from an ancient house, across an expanse of snow-patched pastures shimmering in the sun, toward a crowning tall hill. From the top of the hill—a low mountain, really—one imagines you could see the known world—or at least the known Piedmont, and on the western horizon, the snowy wave of the Blue Ridge. Near the house, fringed by trees, is a family cemetery. Corky's forbearers and the slaves who served them are buried there together. Corky himself is not a young man, and after a distinguished life of farming and of teaching at Woodberry Forest School, after his unswerving community service and leadership of the Virginia Farm Bureau, he will someday join his kinsmen and lie down there with the members of two races. Despite his age, farming continues here. Corky, who has seen on this one swath of land the gamut of techniques and crops, of hand and machine labor, of livestock and heavy equipment as they have evolved, does much, if not most of that farming, himself.

On a winter's day, from a bone-warming farmhouse in which his wife serves steaming tea, Corky will go out to work—because there are animals to be tended to—in the patchy snow. A soft-spoken, erudite man—the sort of farmer Jefferson's fertile mind must have envisioned, a man on top of community and farm issues, a public servant vested in his land—Corky might just be reading Wordsworth or Milton after dinner tonight. It was English Literature that he taught at Woodberry. Why teach? Because, as with many farmers, it was good to have another source of income. Like many farmers in central Virginia, the Corky Shackleford you meet is a far cry from the rustic yeoman of the soil you may have imagined.

For the uninitiated, farmers, like farming itself, can be full of such startling surprises. That the land and the people who work it are redolent with history has never been more evident than in this mosaic of earth we call central Virginia.

THE CODE OF THE COUNTRY

I f the weight of the past mantles this region, giving all who live here a shared story; if the extraordinary achievements of that history set a high bar for the present day, casting a kind of mental shadow— "Yes, here I am, but greatness, true greatness, has walked this same terrain before me"—then it's also true that every day is new, that time has hurtled on, and that people have generally adapted to the quickening pace of life in the 21st Century.

In central Virginia, for all that's come before, the present—with all its critical mass of material and human resources—is uncommonly dynamic. The headlong pace of modernity, the e-revolution and globalization, the fading away of Southern customs that prized civility and a leisurely pace—all have conspired to challenge what once was an unshakable code of conduct: a set of largely unspoken rules; the little (and big) things we do to get along with each other.

That said, it's a mistake to make too much of how much the code has evolved beneath the glitzy surface of change. The backroads farmer may have her cell phone, her own snazzy website, even her iPod; she may have her Masters of Agriculture degree from "that other school" (VPI&SU, which just happens to have a world-renowned livestock and forestry faculty) down in Blacksburg; she may be cutting deals two thousand miles away—or eight thousand, in a foreign market—and telling her husband, over a glass of Chardonnay from a local vineyard, just how she pulled the damn thing off.

But the next day, a fine Sunday morning, may find her at a country church, where generations of her people are buried, way down a bumpy road. Where much of the old Code—if we may capitalize that word—continues to be observed. Where time-worn values are honored and rules of conduct lived by, just as they are when two oncoming pickup trucks brake to a full stop in the middle of a rural public road, and farmers linked by mutual adversity commiserate with each other. Just as they are when folks gather in the county seat, and let their views be known—in a civil way, mind you—about a proposed new forestry land use taxation scheme, as occurred in Orange County in 2006.

Things change, but they stay the same. Only a paradox of that sort can explain why the crucial tenets of the Code to be found anywhere in rural Virginia are still rooted in the rhythms of human interaction with nature. Which—for all the new technological devices, and all the social change—remains the fundamental grounding of all rural Virginia culture.

Respect for nature's ways, and the human effort to work with nature, is at the core of the Code. Almost mystically—for people can be mystical about the place they've long called home—this respect embraces the land itself. The way it "lays," as rural people say, with barely disguised affection. The way it sparkles when the sun rises. The way that particular sycamore juts a bony arm out over the river, like some sylvan hitchhiker.

Respect for people, of course, is the other major tenet of the Code. But what's important to remember is that such respect erodes quickly if other human beings are perceived not to respect nature or the land. One can see that phenomenon readily when a developer callously disfigures the landscape; rural folks who've lived in a place a long time reserve the dregs of their most scathing condemnation for conduct tantamount with "rape." Private landowners new to rural communities risk permanent offense if what they do to their property appears tone deaf to nature and sound land stewardship.

Respect for people has another major aspect in the Code: the drop-of-the-hat willingness to help your neighbor. Those unwilling to pitch in to help others violate the Code as surely as lovesick King David violated more than one of the Ten Commandments. Though rural Virginians take pride in their independence and self-sufficiency, helping your neighbor when she's in real need is a cardinal rule of conduct carved into native Virginia stone.

As is respect for hard work. Those who work on farms day in and day out know just how grueling that work can be. Long hours, adverse weather, and the pace of keeping up with crops, livestock, and markets make agricultural work as demanding as any high-powered, white-collar job in a city—perhaps more so. As the Code sees it, according respect to farmers who accomplish work of that magnitude is not optional. One Rockbridge County newcomer who observed her neighbors at work clearly "gets" the Code. Retiree Linda Hogan (whom we met earlier) told the *Roanoke Times,* "People that are in farming work harder than anyone else I've ever seen. It's a twenty-four hour job."

There is one aspect of the Code can be a real land mine for newcomers: Any whiff of superiority to the culture earns zero tolerance and instant rejection. Newcomers with impressive professional credentials, advanced degrees or conspicuous bankrolls best not "pull rank" on folks hailing from the region.

To do so is to betray "attitude" about things local.

If you remember nothing else, remember this: Rural culture is the great leveler. The most respected citizens are not those with the highest professional or educational pedigree, impeccable grammar or a subscription to the *New York Times,* but those who modestly or even immodestly know how to do things—how to get things done. The local mechanic with a ninth-grade education who can fix anything (particularly seriously stressed farm equipment when a farmer's in a real pinch) virtually walks on water. His work is critically important to the success of the community; and while he knows this is true...his pride never shows.

Elitists who bring their cars to the local mechanic best check their noses-in-the-air at the garage door. Snobs who subscribe to the theory that rural taste is as tacky as a Vegas wedding chapel need not apply for the always-vacant office of High Commissioner of Cultural Taste. Regardless of what wine they pour or how many operas they've seen in Vienna, they'll be lucky not to be run out of the county on the sharp end of a bull.

If you remember nothing else, remember this: RURAL CULTURE IS THE GREAT LEVELER.

None of this is to say that newcomers aren't welcome to reveal their accomplishments, but that is best done slowly. Unlike in many urban circles—where selling oneself with rapid-fire verbal skills can be the key to fast-lane success—the Code of the countryside stresses "what-can-do," not "what-can-say." Flaunting your wisdom, or credentials, or your ability to get things done twice as fast as these slow-talking bumpkin locals, will sure-as-the-day-is-long estrange you from the community.

By contrast, if you're down-to-earth and approach people with the attitude that maybe—just maybe—you have just as much to learn as you do to teach, natives will warm to that modesty, and to your willingness to stretch yourself out of your urban skin. Many of them, after all, are remarkably accomplished as well—perhaps not in the same form as you. This is *their* Code of conduct. You've chosen to move to a place where that Code has kept the peace—and kept neighbors civil—for a very long time.

One additional facet of the Code is involvement in the life of the community. Rural folks are intimately connected with each other, arguably more so than people in suburbs and urban cores. Not only does everyone know everyone else, but everyone is sorely needed to contribute: whether it's manning the volunteer fire department, or helping with a blood or school fund drive, or serving as "poll watcher" on election day.

Jim Turpin and his wife Sally moved from Arlington, Virginia to Nelson County a few years ago, and they hit the ground running. "As soon as you can," Jim advises newcomers, "you need to integrate yourself into the community. Don't be shy—get to know people. Get involved. Try to help."

That's great advice. But this caveat as you get involved is offered to newcomers by Dean and Susan Vidal, who moved from the city to Madison County: "Don't be surprised to hear some bitterness; it's not aimed at you personally. Recognize that many children of farmers cannot afford to buy houses and land in their own counties, near their families, because of upward pressure on prices from affluent newcomers."

One native offers a somewhat ominous variation on this theme of resentment: "Initially, newcomers were well-received. Over time, old-time residents have become more cautious because of issues that develop with new residents."

But don't be discouraged. The overwhelmingly positive experiences of newcomers like the Vidals and the Turpins prove that community needs soon trump native wariness. Out in the country, where the views are bountiful but money is much harder to come by, government funds—local, state, or national—never flow quite as liberally: the list of community needs is endless. People are expected to wear many hats, and to serve if asked. A sparser population—and a scantier government largesse—require more closely knitted cooperation and a willingness to volunteer for the community good. This is a key reality of the Code that newcomers ignore at their peril. In the long run, to refuse to be a "joiner" brands a newcomer as a self-centered outsider—someone who's all too happy to take, but who doesn't bestir himself to pitch in. You don't have to be a farmer to be a community player, but you do have to play.

Life in a rural area is anything but anonymous; whatever you do — or just as significantly, don't do — ripples across the community pond, touching everyone, inviting everyone to assess who you are and what you are made of.

Certainly, no one can stop you from living the sequestered life, up in your new castle on the hill—and enjoying that lovely view, the one that may be the major reason you moved here. But, alas, the view natives have of you will not be quite so "lovely." Gracious as they certainly can be, especially at the beginning, when they will suspend their doubts and give you every chance—your decision to live apart, to be an island in a community that has useful work to do, will not sit well. You'll be "an ugly American" among rural Americans — where life is never easy. Where the needs of educating kids, and taking care of elders, and hanging on to hallowed family land are always crying out for help. You'll be that "ambassador from the city" who just doesn't "get it." You'll be the foreigner who doesn't give a damn. Remember John Donne? "No man is an island…" Out here, the meaningful life — the rewarding life — is a life where you not only enjoy that great view but also make at least some small yet significant positive difference in the lives of the people around you.

Don't relish that sort of life? Well, to each his own — the last time we checked, it's still a free country. But then this agrarian slice of it — in all honesty — just isn't a place where you're likely to be a happy camper. There's a Code here, just as there's a Code in New Zealand, or Scotland, or any other surpassingly beautiful rural landscape you might have chosen to move into. You can choose to ignore that Code — but would you ignore it in a foreign land? If you were so bold as to purchase land on the south island of New Zealand — land as picturesque and fantasy-rich as any rural land on Earth — would you choose to live apart from New Zealand's local customs? New Zealand is a land of sheep, and sheep farmers; a pastoral paradise that, like rural Virginia, confronts rapidly changing times. Would you feel unhappy in a rural New Zealand culture, as native New Zealanders try their damndest to keep that rural culture alive?

We have our doubts. We think you're "attuned." We think you "get it."

One final aspect of the Code merits special consideration:
Traditional land usage.

L and is sacred in rural culture. It has been that way for what may seem forever, for it's the wealth of the land by which people have prospered. That land is finite. As country folks are quick to tell you, you can't make any more of it. As a result, just as basketball coaches tell their players how crucial it is to "value the basketball" on each possession and not turn over the ball to the other team, rural landowners value land as they do no other material possession.

Add to this the sanctity of private property rights. The facts—that land is sacred and of utmost value, and that property rights are the crucial guardians of a landowner's property—are intertwined ideas. For prosperity to continue, rural landowners believe that—to the reasonable extent possible—*they*, not the government, should decide how their land is used. The idea that any coercive force—whether it be new governmental restrictions or, for that matter, the potentially differing views of some newcomers—could erode private property rights, is anathema to rural culture.

Ironically, perhaps—because they love their land dearly—this helps explain why the vast majority of rural landowners in Virginia are adamantly opposed to any restrictions that would make their property harder to sell. As one native put it, "Sometimes long-time residents want the ability to develop their land; that land may be their primary equity." For good reason, too: kidneys do fail; medical care is not yet free, and rural folks still try to pay what they owe.

"Land," remarked another native, "is an asset to farmers, the major asset for most of us. Newcomers need to understand this."

Even Corky Shackleford—whose land goes back in the family to 1817, and a man who personifies the phrase "loving your family land"—wants no part of restrictions that would make the option of selling that land more difficult. Newcomers, Corky told us, often don't seem to comprehend how a farmer could so forcibly defend his right to be the master of his own property. As Corky sees it, they tend to view his open farmland as essentially community property—to be enjoyed, visually at least, by all.

In a sense, they're right—but not in the "keep things bucolic" sense meant by many newcomers. Its subtlety makes this idea not an easy one to grasp—but there *is* a sense in rural communities that private open land is also held in common; that it belongs, in an almost familial sense, to the "family" of community residents.

There's a complicated paradox here: Yes, land belongs to its owner, absolutely and irrevocably. It's the owner who chooses what to do with it; the owner decides who is welcome on his property. However, as long as the land and its owner isn't disturbed, private property has often been available for use by community members. In essence, the Code says: Don't shut out someone you know who's also a trustworthy person. As long as there's a prior understanding, a person living in the community is often welcome to walk, or ride a horse or ATV, or maybe even hunt or fish, on privately-owned land.

That said, a newcomer should never assume that it's okay to use a

neighbor's land the way a mountain-climber might climb a mountain—
"because it's there." Farmers and other rural landowners tend to be on red
alert for newcomers wandering uninvited on their property. With good reason.
Reports are legion of newcomers being lured by the beauty of an open field, a
sparkling stream—assuming, naively, and without malice—that such beautiful
places deserve their company. This won't be a farmer's perspective. Though our
farmer may also think her property beautiful, and she is drawn to that open
space, too, our farmer is also conducting business on that land. Maybe she is
raising cattle; maybe trying to harvest an alfalfa crop. The sight of a newcomer
(perhaps with pets) waltzing across an open pasture —while a bull lurks in a
far corner—is likely to bring out the bull in the farmer. Seeing that newcomer,
she'll see red.

The best advice is the most obvious: Always ask. And long before you ask,
earn your right to ask by working to earn the landowner's trust. Spend some
time. Show some genuine interest in the farmer's operation. Offer to help
any chance you get—even the smallest forms of help count for a lot as natives
gauge whether you have the right stuff. It's all doable. None of these good will
gestures are rocket science.

One story will illustrate. We know a newcomer who enjoys a
large pond on his property, where he loves to retreat to go fishing and read great
novels (he favors Tolstoy and Camus). One recent summer, his neighbor—a
taciturn, extremely hard-working woman who personifies the "dawn to dark"
farmer's life—was trying to grow row crops of vegetables in what was becoming a
severe drought…and things weren't getting any better. As one Blue Ridge farmer
likes to say at such times, looking up ruefully at yet another cloudless sky: "You
know, it don't rain in dry weather." The woman's struggling crops proved it.

She had her pride—and she'd never really had much to do with the newcomer.
He'd kept to himself, and it was a pretty safe bet he wasn't aware that she had a
looming crisis. It's also a pretty safe bet that she wasn't conversant with the nuances
of Tolstoy and Camus. But she swallowed her pride—and went to see him.

Not long after that, an impressive assemblage of irrigation pipes brought
water from the newcomer's pond to the farmer's row crops. The farmer got her
water, and the literature-lover got to know one of those "country people" Tolstoy
wrote about so often…**and he also got, without asking, a lifetime supply of
whichever vegetable was perfectly ripe.**

It's a fun story—and it tells us just how simple it can be, really, to break through the cultural divide. But violating the property code itself is a serious offense. Either: (1) not respecting the rights of property owners, or (2) shutting out trustworthy neighbors, is a social felony, not a misdemeanor. It's for this reason that the newcomer who buys private property customarily used by community residents—and then gates it off, with "in-your-face" signage—risks the sort of opprobrium reserved in the Old West for cattle rustlers.

Terry Silber, a farmer in Maine, put the matter succinctly in her thoughtful book, *A Small Farm in Maine*. "I have seen many new landowners move into their homesteads and tack up KEEP OUT and NO TRESPASSING signs. These signs have always struck me as extremely hostile and arrogant. They disregard the history of the land's use by the community, and they are such a visible way of imposing values by virtue of economic advantage." Silber's reference to "economic advantage"—i.e., that the folks putting up the signs tend to be wealthier than their neighbors, and are flaunting that wealth—has the ring of truth. In his classic *Democracy in America*, published in 1835, Alexis de Tocqueville might well have called such behavior un-American. "In the United States," Toqueville observed, "the more opulent citizens take great care not to stand aloof from the people; on the contrary, they constantly keep on easy terms with the lower classes; they listen to them, they speak to them every day."

Unless you have the stomach for it, you just don't want to be seen as Public Enemy Number One. Few people do. That's why your approach to the private property code will go a long way toward determining your credibility in your new community.

Agricultural Economics 101

N ow, imagine we're back in the classroom — scratched-up desktops, scent of chalk and Pine Sol, preferably with a nice view out the classroom window. We've talked about Jefferson, his vision, experimental agriculture, husbandry, and financial troubles. We've talked about the perennial challenges that farmers face. We've touched on financially successful farmers, the ones who've mastered the game, captured markets, figured out how to endure. We've given you some context, some background, to help illuminate some of the darker corners of rural and farm culture.

Now that we are all chest-deep with our farmer neighbors, trying to keep our heads above water, let's get a bit more specific and discuss some facts and figures.

First, the sobering national picture: Since 1910, America has lost two-thirds of its farms; in the 1930s, twenty-five percent of the population lived on farms — now, it's less than two percent. Though there remain some 921 million acres in farmland in the United States, we're losing that farmland at a rate only a bulldozer could love. Just two examples: between 1992 and 1997, we lost fourteen million farmland acres nationally. That's not pretty. Since 2002 alone, North Carolina has lost 300,000 acres of farmland, and since 1964 that state has lost an astounding 37 percent of its farmland to urbanization.

Farm loss rates differ from state to state. Though not among the top ten states suffering losses, Virginia was down from 8,753,625 acres in 1997 to 8,624,829 acres in 2002, a one percent drop in five years. During that same period, the number of Virginia farms decreased by four percent, down to 47,606. Essentially, these alarming national and regional trends continue unabated.

So we ask: Will the day come when we no longer have enough farmland to meet our needs for food and forest products? Citizen involvement and county ordinances with teeth are crucial: In 1994 Augusta County drew up a comprehensive plan to set aside areas for agriculture and areas for growth — then failed to pass laws to enforce that plan. The result: land designated for farm preservation in the plan is being steadily eroded by subdivisions.

Dr. Royce Hanson, a political scientist retired from American University and chairman of the Montgomery County Planning Board of the Maryland-National Capital Parks and Planning Commission, has been active for nearly thirty years in efforts to preserve farmland. "It's inevitable," he told us, "that some farmland will be converted as the country grows. But I think there's a growing sense that we can't continue from an energy point of view, from an environmental quality perspective, from transportation and housing costs, to continue to spread in the way that we have in the past."

But "spread" we continue to do. Yet, despite these menacing trends, farm efficiency nationwide is exemplary—a model for the world—and food remains relatively cheap. Americans spend roughly ten percent of their disposable income on food—a figure we should all celebrate. In many countries, it's fifty percent or more. And ours is the cleanest, healthiest food in the world.

Contrary to what we might assume—that farming has become marginalized in the brave new world of high tech industries—agriculture's contribution to the national economy remains enormous. Twenty-five million Americans—seventeen percent of the workforce—participate in some form of agriculture—growing, processing, distributing.

SEEMS IMPROBABLE, BUT IT'S TRUE:

Taken together, our food and forest products industries are America's largest employers.

Overall, agriculture weighs in at thirteen percent of our nation's worth, a figure that conclusively demonstrates just how crucial are our farmer neighbors to the nation's financial health.

But we don't make the bottom line easy for them. Wrap your mind around these numbers: In the 1960s farmers could buy land at an average of $500 an acre; today the national average when buying farmland is $2000 an acre. Between 1948 and 2004, agricultural commodity prices rose at less than half the rate of inflation, while farmers' share of a consumer's food dollar has fallen from 31 cents in 1980 to 19 cents in 2002. Only extraordinary leaps in technology and productivity have allowed American farmers to keep up—breathlessly, you might say, because farmers are also working harder and longer.

Sadly, though, many of them have not kept up. Today we have 300,000 fewer farmers than we did in the 1980s. Which wasn't so long ago. 300,000—that's another number that's hard to wrap your mind around, until you see their faces. Until you see how, one by one, some photographer in the family took photographs of each one of them leaving that farm behind. Putting up a "FOR SALE" sign. Getting in the truck, and looking back—just once—and driving on down the road, when the sale closed.

In some counties in central Virginia, the figures are a bit more encouraging. Despite its failure to enact laws to implement farm preservation, Augusta County actually increased its farm acreage from 1997 to 2002, though the number of farms declined—part of a national trend toward fewer farms with larger acreages. Happily—at least for Jefferson's vision of a nation of small farmers—Rockbridge County has resisted this trend, actually increasing its number of farms from 631 in 2002 to 789 in 2003, in part a result of the breakup of large land parcels into smaller farming enterprises.

What's happened in Rockbridge County offers a window into an encouraging trend across other regions of Virginia as well as the nation: a partial transition to "niche" farming. Though Rockbridge remains strong in traditional forms of agriculture—ranking tenth in the state in beef cattle production, tenth in alfalfa and eleventh in hay production—niche faming has emerged as an important component of the county's economy. Non-traditional farm products such as garlic, fish, alpacas, Christmas trees, and many other commodities are helping stem farmland loss by providing new sources of income for farm families.

Talk to Steve Murray—whose gracefully sloping farm on the outskirts of Charlottesville offers, among its products, earth-dark compost that nourishes many a garden—and you have a vivid picture of the direction many farmers must go to stay in business. Changes in the agricultural economy as well as environmental, labor and other issues have made it clear to veteran farmers like Steve—a man as passionate about farming as anyone could possibly be—that what's required now is farm diversification and "thinking outside the box," devising new concepts and strategies that generate non-traditional farming income.

For Steve—a Renaissance man himself who knows how to construct buildings, repair engines, build up new markets from scratch, and easily hold his own intellectual ground in debate—learning how to "grow" the mounds of compost laid out in rows along his farm's ridge has pointed the way to non-traditional success. That idea worked, just as successfully as the brainstorm Steve had to open up part of his farm to uses like Atlantic Coast Conference running events. As Steve sees it, for many farmers to succeed now, they must yield to creative adaptation, finding the right niches even if some of them—like running events—are not necessarily about production agriculture.

Meeting a farmer like Steve Murray you realize, despite all the bad news, why we will always have farmers in the manner Jefferson envisioned. Some of them—the creative risk-takers, the "outside-the-boxers"—will find ingenious ways to use their land, protect their way of life, *and* move the economy forward. As Jefferson hoped, they'll be cultural leaders, decision-makers, people with a diverse range of talents who know what the world needs next. Stewards of the earth, they are.

Whether in the state as a whole or central Virginia in particular, none of this is to suggest that traditional farm commodities are freefalling in economic importance. Certainly tobacco—grown as early in Virginia as 1612 by John Rolfe—is no longer key to the state's fortunes, though Virginia still ranks fifth, nationally, in tobacco production. Yet top livestock items like beef cattle and dairy cows, broilers and turkeys, and crops like soybeans and corn still account for the vast majority of farm income, which according to the 2002 Census of Agriculture amounted in Virginia to $2.4 billion from farms averaging 181 acres in size. In that same census, livestock and poultry sales more than doubled those of crops, underscoring the importance of traditional Old MacDonald's Farm critters like hogs and pigs, cattle and sheep.

Indeed, from one end of the Old Dominion to the other, agricultural products—some traditional, some relatively new to the state—weigh in on an impressive scale. Production of apples, fresh tomatoes, wine grapes and Christmas trees, as well as the enterprises of aquaculture and horse farming, all have ranked in the top ten, nationally, in the past few years. Agriculturally, ours is a state playing a significant national role.

Farming's economic significance can obscure its more elemental importance: as the source of our food. A road sign on Interstate 70 in central Kansas drives home the point: "One Kansas farmer feeds you and 128 other people." As motorists whiz by on the arrow-straight highway, it's doubtful that many pause in their high-speed cocoons to reflect on the self-propelled combines and

grain storage silos visible in the distance, or on the farmers who work in those immense fields and lonesome clusters of farm buildings. This is "flyover country"—the core of the Heartland, the geographical center of the nation; to New Yorkers and Left Coasters and other urban fast-laners, the Heartland is known only by a cursory glance out the airplane window at a cruising altitude of 30,000 feet. What happens 30,000 feet below is what feeds the cities and suburbs of our Nation; sadly, these urban folks are so divorced from the sources of their food supply that they might as well be sourcing their meals from the moon.

There's a cruel fact of life here: Without food, we die—or, getting just a sliver of it, we hang by a thread. See: major swaths of Africa. See: Bangladesh. See even: America, where shocking numbers of people go hungry. Without those Kansas farmers—and their counterparts in Virginia and elsewhere—Americans unskilled in producing food themselves would soon be like wild animals driven from their habitat by urban encroachment, like bears foraging for food in suburban garbage cans.

Sound harsh? Well, food is so basic, we're better served by being starkly real about it. It comes from *places*, very specific places—like that farm down the road. It comes from *people* who grow it—people sorely tempted to sell out to developers who are offering them top dollar. We must support in their efforts those people who nurture our food along, and defend their farmland. We must assume our share of the responsibility for maintaining what is currently, at least, a remarkably reliable and safe food supply.

But we—consumers of food—could say: These people, and the land they produce the food on, really don't mean all that much to us, actually, now that you mention it. We don't know these people. We don't socialize with them on Saturday nights. Their politics, their religion, their freckle-faced kids are—well, you know. They're different. Truth to tell, we really don't have anything in common with them. If they sell their land, and subdivisions pop up like skunk cabbage because they can no longer make a living from that land—well, that's the American way. Harsh? Yes. Sort of Darwinian, when you think about it. Every man for himself. Not my problem.

To make that latter choice—which, despite our better natures, all too many of us do—is self-destructive. No good can come of it. Nor, in a society where consumer access and convenience is king, can any good come of undermining farmers whose livelihood depends on their ability to ship their products long distance. As encouraging and important as the booming "local food" phenomenon is, where consumers interact with and learn about farmers, where food is fresh and energy costs are dramatically reduced—it's also true that farmland, wherever it is, *stays* farmland whenever its products can be profitably delivered to markets. That's a huge net plus. Local and "long distance" food each have their role. Which leads us to reiterate that most fundamental of points:

"The understanding of what it takes to run a profitable farm is somewhat lacking among newcomers" says Dr. Martha Walker, in the *Roanoke Times*. Martha's a woman determined to do whatever it takes to create true communities mingling natives and newcomers—she is the Community Viability Specialist we met earlier. Here, she speaks nothing but the truth. Why would newcomers understand, at least initially? It's the nature of our segregated cultural experience, which creates those barriers we're trying, in this book, to break down. We appreciate your staying with us so far. So, to put it a tad more saltily than Dr. Walker:

> Farmers aren't farming to get their jollies. Farming's a business. It is true that farms do provide a wide variety of environmental and aesthetic benefits to society at large. They're great for recharging groundwater aquifers, great for reducing rainwater runoff and potential flooding, great for providing habitat for birds and a host of four-footed animals. But beneath it all, the bottom line is profit. Farms are not public parks.

So, unless you're a "cappuccino cowboy"—as one "hobbyist" livestock farmer who lives within three miles of a Lawrence, Kansas Starbucks merrily calls himself—you're playing Monopoly with real money. For most farmers, farming is the sole or major source of their income. It is never easy to profit from farming. Overhead costs of equipment, rising property taxes, debt interest, labor, property maintenance, marketing, agricultural inputs and more can be as sobering as a river threatening to flood.

Certainly, what meets a newcomer's eye can be deceptive: Assumptions about the rip-roaring wealth of farmers—based on land and buildings and livestock and crops a newcomer may eyeball from the highway—badly miss the mark. Not to put too fine a point on it, but assuming farmers are rolling in cash is sort of like assuming that the façades of a Hollywood studio back lot are the real McCoy.

In his masterful book *Farm: A Year in the Life of an American Farmer,* Pulitzer Prize-winning author Richard Rhodes examines the lives—and finances—of a Missouri farm family working land they own (with a mortgage) totaling 337 acres and land they lease totaling 779 acres. For Tom Bauer, eighteen-hour workdays during the growing and harvest seasons are routine. At the end of a typical year, Tom, his wife Sally, and their three teenaged children (at least one of whom, they hope and pray, will join them after college on the farm) sit down together and do the math.

Gross income for the year (this was the late 1980s) from hogs, calves, corn, wheat, and soybeans—with some depreciation figured in—comes to $152,090. Total expenses for the year come to $117,608, for a net gain of $34,482. But when they Bauers factor in income and Social Security self-employment taxes, they realize they've cleared about $19,000 for the year.

$19,000. Eighteen hour days. Could you do it? Would you?

All too succinctly, Rhodes sums up how the Bauers feel about their enterprise. "Farming was a good life, but it didn't make you rich."

To the starry-eyed observer, the idea that farming is a business—and not just fodder for picturesque, pastoral-themed calendars—comes to a friction point when we think about how farms preserve open space. Open space: If ever a newcomer's heart will beat more rapidly, it might just be at the sight of unspoiled open space. And why not? That's a commodity in short supply back in Megalopolis.

Farms create this visual magic, of course. By farming instead of developing the living daylights out of their property, farmers perform what can aptly be called a public service. Real estate agents know all about it—the value of property rises or falls based on the quality of its "viewshed." Throw up a bristling cluster of new tract houses in that viewshed and its quality tanks. So does the illusion that one has escaped the city to an idyllic landscape.

SUPPORT FOR AGRICULTURE BY NEWCOMERS IS OFTEN DRIVEN MORE BY SUPPORT FOR OPEN SPACE THAN BY SUPPORT FOR FARMING.

To no one's surprise, there's trouble here in River City —just listen to the natives. As one told us, "Support for agriculture by newcomers is often driven more by support for open space than by support for farming." Another native said: "Some new land-owners have a commitment to land preservation/conservation/open space or easements—but not necessarily to agriculture."

There's an interesting story that dramatizes what can happen when a farmer and a newcomer appraise the same chunk of land—one view from Mars, the other from Venus. The story is told by Hank Will, a soft-spoken, former biology professor with a Ph.D. from the University of Chicago—who re-careered to become editor of that venerable country lifestyle magazine, *Grit*. We had a chance to talk with Hank in Topeka, Kansas, to which he recently moved, having lived many years in New Hampshire. A part-time farmer as well as *Grit* editor, with a family background in seed sales and grain farming in North Dakota, Hank is attuned to the sort of problems that can arise when two cultures aren't even in the same public library, much less on the same page.

"I knew a farmer in New Hampshire," Hank told us, speaking softly as Teddy Roosevelt with his big stick, "who discovered a way to make ends meet by leasing some of his pasture ground for a cellphone microwave tower. Now maybe I don't want to have a cell phone microwave tower in my pasture, my back yard, but if the income makes sense, it's sort of like, yeah, that's a way to put your land to work.

"Well several of his neighbors took him to court, because they had five-acre plots near him. And the cell tower was ruining their view, in their minds detracting from the value of the large houses they had built. They were new-comers moving in from the outside, and their argument was: the whole reason they had moved there in the first place was the beautiful view of his pasture. My question is: 'Did any of them offer to pay him for their beautiful view of his pasture?' To a person who farms full-time, land is an asset from which you can earn income. You might love it, and you might think it's beautiful as well, but at the end of the day, if it doesn't pay you, you can't stay there."

Hank didn't tell us the outcome of the litigation against the farmer. How you feel about that outcome will reveal a great deal about how far you've stretched, culturally, in your new rural home.

But the question Hank asks about the newcomers offering to pay for their view of the farmer's pasture lands a knockout punch. From where a farmer sits on her John Deere, it's a perfectly valid question: Why shouldn't they pay? In fact, if the tower has to come down, why shouldn't they pay a sum equal to the amount garnered from leasing his land for the tower? For that matter, if the view of his pasture is *that* blissful an experience for them—maybe it even lowers their blood pressure by twenty percent!—why shouldn't they also pay an additional share of the costs of maintaining it as a pasture?

Now we admit, that last question borders on the provocative. But it does underscore a point. Wouldn't it have helped, early on, before the farmer signed the lease agreement with the telephone company, if the newcomers had ventured out of their big houses and knocked on the farmer's door and said, "Thank you, sir, for your pasture. It means the world to us. Without it, our lives would have so much less beauty in them every day."

And wouldn't it have helped if these same "view-huggers" (to coin a phrase) had then said, "What can we do to be good neighbors? How can we all understand each other's needs and help each other out?" And if they had said: "Your pasture means so much to us, maybe there's a way we can help you maintain that pasture. Get the hay up. Help spread the fertilizer. Babysit your youngest child when you and your wife are out in the pasture working. Any job you can think of."

Perhaps it would have made no difference. Maybe the farmer would have gawked at these strange characters on his porch and thought, "Man, these city slickers moving out here in droves are getting nuttier every year."

But maybe not. And maybe when the time came to lease some land for a tower he might have found—if he had one—a less intrusive site.

We'll never know. Not the lawyers, in the court case. Not the judge or jury.

What we do know—what Hank's story drives home—is that farmland benefits everyone living close by…and not just by preserving open space. Farmers do love the land they work. As Richard Rhodes writes about Tom Bauer in the book *Farm*, "Tom doubted if anyone who wasn't born on a farm could understand how he felt about the land. 'Why hell,' they'd say, 'It's just a piece of dirt.'

It was more than that to him. He knew every piece of it and how it lay and its problems and all. But he couldn't explain it and he didn't see how anyone could understand it who hadn't lived it."

Because of that love (with very rare exceptions) farmers are good environmental stewards—a quality that ripples across the whole neighborhood. Though organic farming has many virtues, you don't have to be growing your crops or raising your livestock organically to practice sustainable farming.

STEWARDSHIP—a public service—can be accomplished in a variety of ways, and farmers have every incentive to practice sound stewardship. When controlling weeds and invasive species, farmers go out of their way to protect environmentally beneficial plants. When applying what are always extremely expensive pesticides, they do so only when necessary and only after rigorous training that qualifies them as registered pesticide applicators. Improper application can lead to the loss of an applicator's license—or worse. When storing or composting or spreading manure, farmers know what they're doing. The environmental longevity of their farm depends on sound stewardship. The economic viability of every farm depends on it. The possibility of passing on land that they love to a child or grandchild depends on it. The high stakes of what are sometimes called "best management practices"—reducing erosion and runoff, keeping soil fertile—are always in their minds. Again: No one cares as much about topsoil as the family that owns it. Topsoil to a farmer is like hay in the barn, like cash in the bank.

FORESTRY

THAT "OTHER" AGRICULTURE

Before we leave our (just slightly musty) "Ag Econ 101" classroom, let's have a word about that "other" kind of farming in Virginia: growing and harvesting trees. More than 300,000 private landowners own and control seventy-seven percent of the forest land in Virginia, meaning that—subject to state laws governing timber-cutting practices—private landowners bear the lion's share of responsibility for sound forest management. Praise or curse all we will about how the U.S. Forest Service administers National Forests in the state, or how the locals were forced to cede gobs of private forest land to the Feds when Shenandoah National Park was formed...the fate of forests and of local ecosystems dependent on forests rests mostly in the hands of people like—well, us. Tree-hugger, forest marauder or something in between...Where do you fall on that spectrum? Where do we? With so much at stake, it's small wonder that folks can get as bent out of shape about trees as trees themselves in a windstorm.

For newcomers—and, for that matter, for some natives—the "train wreck" of land being "cut over" and the raggedy, trashed look of what trees (or maybe just stumps) remain, can be profoundly disturbing. Trees, and tree-cutting, bring out great depths of emotion in people. Joyce Kilmer expressed this intensity famously: "I think that I shall never see/A poem lovely as a tree..." And some would argue that no matter in how aesthetically-minded a manner a forest is timbered, the result becomes an eyesore for some time to come. (In this regard, the untrained eye can be deceiving. After all, when timbering done in an environmentally sound way—which can include both selective and clear-cutting—isn't that a "beautiful" thing, to do the right thing for healthy forest succession *and* the right thing in providing jobs and forest products?)

To be sure, environmental damage can—we emphasize that word *can*—be done. Soil erosion on steep slopes. Silt in streams. Habitat displacement—these and other environmental wounds, aggravated by "slash and trash" techniques that evade the watchful eye of forestry officials—are all possible. Harvesting timber is invasive surgery. With care, the ultimate outcome can and should be a "win-win," both for the environment and for the wallet, but it's hard to "see the forest for the trees" when once-proud giants lie fallen on the earth like the dead at Gettysburg.

As a forester with the Virginia Department of Forestry, Mike Santucci works "on the ground" in Madison, Greene, and Rappahannock counties. "There are a lot of misconceptions about logging," Mike told us. "A lot of people move here because they think it's the Garden of Eden. They'll see timber being cut and the first words they'll say are, 'Restrictions.' Next, 'regulations.' They may not understand that while we do have laws, there is a right to practice proper forestry in Virginia."

"What people often don't understand," according to Mike, "is that land has to be profitable if it's the source of your income. You have to allow it to be profitable, because that's what's keeping the land open and not developed. It's also a misconception that the natural world is a static system. If you see a seventy-year-old oak stand, you might easily think that it's always been seventy years old. Well, no. Maybe once, that was an open, recently logged space" … 70 years ago.

From newcomers, Mike receives his share of angry phone calls. "There's a difference," he told us, "in perceptions, or paradigms. With the locals it's kind of, 'Those damn New Yorkers, they're nature virgins.' With the newcomers it's, 'Those damn rednecks.' In general," he said, "newcomers tend to be more politically liberal. More environmentally sensitive. They tend toward restricting everything they don't like. Folks who've lived here a long time tend to be more conservative. They favor economic incentives for land use, if possible. They believe in property rights. All this cultural friction is part of a big picture: making a living versus natural beauty. But the best tool, really, is not regulation, but allowing people to make a living. That keeps the land open. But people position themselves right out of the gate… and that's hard to overcome."

When trees are slamming to the ground, a typical newcomer call, Mike reports, goes something like this: "My neighbor's logging the woods right next door to me, and destroying everything. How can I shut him down?"

Things can get worse from there—or better. "I try to be upbeat and honest," Mike told us. "If it's a confrontational situation, I try to calm them down. I tell them the owner has a right to log his timber. I tell them logging never looks pretty—silviculture never looks pretty—but here again, nature is not a static system. It's gonna change, no matter if we're a part of that or not. When done well, logging will allow nature to rebuild itself in a way that's beneficial to the environment. Lately, it seems like newcomers are more receptive to learning about that. If I can be with them for half a day, that makes a big difference."

"Taking the heat"—that would be a pretty good working job description for what Mike Santucci does. Just how valuable—for everyone—is a man who can calm people down? Fortunately, Mike seems to be the sort of fellow who can speak the language of both cultures, generating light, not heat, as he explains the rules.

When done well, logging will allow nature to rebuild itself in a way that's beneficial to the environment.

If you're a newcomer and want to learn more about those rules—and about the best practices of logging—what's good, what's not good, when cutting trees—give a forester like Mike a call. Your local forester is very much at your service. Do the same thing if you're observing a logging operation near you that seems in any way adverse to reasonable practices. Foresters like Mike can make a determination and—if necessary, as an officer of the law, crack down on the loggers—even arrest them on the spot. The reality is that there are a few scofflaw loggers out there—tree-rustlers, you might call them—stealing from the environment if not necessarily from the landowner. The Virginia Department of Forestry is also a great resource for information about Virginia law pertaining to harvesting timber, and for learning about sound forestry management practices you can apply on your own property.

Handled carefully, trees are a renewable resource, and they're a potential source of income on that land you now occupy. Forest trees are true friends—giving us beauty, protecting soil and wildlife, absorbing carbon dioxide and therefore helping to slow global warming, and when we harvest them, putting money in our pockets that helps pay those property taxes and other unfortunate prices of living the good country life!

LIVING THE
COUNTRY
LIFESTYLE

The graybeards among us are old enough to remember a colorful phenomenon of the 1960s and '70s: the "back-to-the-land" movement, when folks raised in cities—most of them young and unabashedly hirsute—reinvented themselves as homesteaders out in the country, gobbling up property and trying their damndest to be farmers. It was a grand, if at times comically madcap, social experiment. The fact that it mostly failed, and that most of the back-to-the-landers morphed into back-to-the-urban-jungle-ers, doesn't diminish the romantic charm of it. When Neil Young sang, "Are you ready for the country?/Well, it's time to go," he spoke for a generation of young Americans who—like today's urban migrants—were looking for something mellower than the urban grind. As things turned out, many of the folks who answered Neil Young's call weren't ready for the country. Few grasped in advance just how relentlessly difficult it is to wrest a living out of the land. But we can learn from their experience.

These days, what motivates urban refugees typically isn't the desire to do serious farming. But what can happen out in the country, farming or no farming, hasn't changed very much. The country is still the country—manure is still manure, and a mudhole after a thunderstorm is still a mudhole after a thunderstorm. The trick—now as it was then—is knowing what to expect, and not going ballistic when things you may have taken for granted back in the city can't be taken for granted anymore. That curbside recycling service that rightly made you feel so virtuous—alas, out here, you'll have to schlep your recyclables to a recycling center. And so it goes.

Some of the natives can be a tad ornery about all this. "People," one of them told us tartly, "want a rural setting but urban services." Another suggested: "They need to understand what newcomers will NOT get in the rural areas. Urban infrastructure is not in place in the rural community."

Dean and Susan Vidal—the folks who moved into Madison County—

offer this broad piece of advice for fellow newcomers: **"Don't import the freneticism of the city, or you will find that you have successfully recreated what you left behind.** Don't expect shopping access to three choices of everything, 24/7, within five miles of your house. Family-run businesses may close at noon on Saturday. Celebrate this, and wait until Monday."

Store business hours—and no Starbucks within easy reach—are one thing. But what the realtor may not tell you is that even the most basic necessities—electricity, for example—might not be available under adverse weather conditions. Anyone moving to the country is well advised to buy a generator well ahead of that next powerful thunder- or ice-storm. When the power goes out, so, typically, does the water. You're on your own, kid…

…and you're a long way from many of the things city folks know are close by when they're needed: as in—we hesitate to bring this up—hospitals! That's a sobering thought if the likelihood is high of an urgent trip to the hospital. Rural counties rustle up rescue squads, of course; but good as they are, there's nothing rescue squads can do to shorten and straighten out that long and winding road into town.

Speaking of roads—there's yet another problematic fact of country life. For starters, after a big snowstorm that road of yours just might be the last one plowed within a five-county radius. That private road snaking its way a quarter-mile up to your house—well, let's see, whose road is that? Remember those obnoxious bumper stickers? "AS A MATTER OF FACT, I DO OWN THE DAMN ROAD!" Exactly right. You own the one on your property, and unless a band of angels descends from the sky to help you plow it after that same snowstorm, you're on your own once again. Maybe that shiny new four-wheel drive vehicle you bought for your new life out here will get you down that road…or maybe it won't. Road maintenance, road repair—after a cloudburst, on your own land you'll learn the full meaning of those phrases. Unless you pave your road, of course—a practical decision, but one that doesn't always score aesthetic points. The point is, it's different out here. You never used to have to worry about such things.

There's a seeming contradiction in all this. By moving to the country you've simultaneously increased your need for self-sufficiency and your need to help—and be helped by—your neighbors. Depending on the situation, either set of needs may apply. When the electricity goes out—and it will, you can bet the farm on it—knowing how to get that generator up and running will come in mighty handy. As will knowing how to sharpen and wield that chainsaw when you've got a doctor's appointment in an hour, and there's a downed oak tree straddling your driveway from that big storm last night.

Being a good neighbor — and having good neighbors — will become more than just warm and fuzzy concepts when that inevitable time arrives when you can't do all the work yourself.

If there's anything more valuable than having a good neighbor out in the country, it would have to be that pot of gold itself at the end of the rainbow. "Good fences," Robert Frost wrote memorably in his poem *Mending Wall*, "make good neighbors." But it's also true that good neighbors make good fences! *[If needed. You might want to read the poem again; neither man owned any livestock.]* But if you do need a fence, that aw-shucks, drawling neighbor who's been putting fences up all his life just might be the man you need to show you how it's done well.

That, and a million other things. Maybe your neighbor has the welding equipment needed to mend that tractor arm you were using with the bush-hog. It's all good — these kind of situations, where people are helping people. Overcoming any reluctance you may have to ask for or accept help will be a first major step in converting that word "stranger" to "friend." Out in the country, independence can be an overrated virtue. Nothing wrong with it in theory — except that *interdependence* is what really brings people much closer together. And interdependence more nearly approximates what nature is all about — a circle of life is which everything needs everything else.

CAUTION: *Asking for advice can be a door-opener to friendship. Expecting daily help should be an employer/employee matter. Asking for help should be reserved for real trouble.*

One of the smartest — yet easiest — moves you can make is to get acquainted with your county Virginia Cooperative Extension agent. Typically there's some concrete reason for doing that — maybe you want to plant some grapevines and make some homemade wine, or maybe you want to set out a backyard orchard but don't know what kind of fruit trees will do well at your site. Maybe you just want to find out what kind of soil you have before you make any further plans. In our experience, it's a rare county agent *[different lingo, same job. —ed.]* who lacks an outgoing, enthusiastic personality. As agents of Virginia's two land-grant universities (Virginia Tech and Virginia State University) one key element of an Extension Agent's job is to be available—free of charge—to citizens with questions about all things agricultural, including professional farmers and folks looking to grow or raise products for home consumption. (Soil testing is free for commercial farmers, but there is a modest fee for non-commercial landowners.)

Talk about a human resource. Wythe Morris, the county agent in Carroll County who also serves as a horticultural specialist in four southwestern Virginia counties, is a walking encyclopedia of agricultural knowledge who typifies the county agent breed across the state: engaging, quick and eager to help upon request, and—in that quintessentially American way—optimistic yet grounded in experience. When a newcomer calls Wythe, he told us, looking for information about her site, Wythe will come out ASAP for a site visit. "I like to do it one-on-one," he said, and if desired, "do soil tests and slope and exposure evaluations, and take detailed notes." Depending on what the landowner wants to accomplish, Wythe will connect her with a Virginia Tech specialist in Blacksburg or Winchester, who will study Wythe's notes, make further evaluations, and, ultimately, make recommendations to the landowner.

"Essentially," Wythe said, "let's say if someone wants to plant some grapes, or maybe some fruit trees, I'm the leading edge for Virginia Tech—I do the first part—and then I'll turn it over to a specialist. Except I don't really turn it all over, because I'm here to help all along the way. Let's say they have insect or disease problems, I'll come out and collect plant samples and find out what the problems are. Deer problems—like with your young fruit trees—the key thing about deer, they're creatures of habit, and you have to find some way to break their habits, whether it's with spray materials as a repellent, or an electronic repellent, like a cougar scream—whatever it is. I'm there for problem-solving down the road."

For folks interested in getting into a somewhat larger scale farming, for profit, Wythe and his colleagues offer classes and one-on-one help in a variety of subjects, from starting a small business to developing a budget, from farm liability issues in agritourism to how to build a fence or a pond. "Farming 101," he calls such services. "Our bottom line is we're here to make sure they're successful."

Newcomers Jim and Sally Turpin looked up the county agent in Nelson County to get advice on selecting a site for planting wine grapes. Before they even bought their property, the agent helped them search for the right place to buy. Every time Jim and Sally drove down from Arlington to look at property, they made a point of stopping in to see the agent, to develop that relationship even further.

In your case, getting to know the county agent is probably the shortest route to learning more about your land and what the possibilities might be, say, for serious gardening or "hobby" farming. As Wythe Morris illustrates, county agents are there for brain-picking—they know not only just about everyone in the county, but also—in a general way—a great deal about everything from plant diseases to alpaca breeding. Experience is on their side—they're a fount of information about what's worked and hasn't worked over the years. This is their turf; and now that it's yours too, it's a county agent's job to work with you as you develop your site. He's not working alone, either. Every Extension agent has the academic and research resources of a major land-grant university available to support his mission; much of this University research and Extension Service information is readily available on a number of land-grant university websites, Virginia Tech being foremost.

Along with the county agent, you might want to get to know a local Master Gardener. Or, join a Master Gardener group. Across Virginia, Wythe told us, most county extension offices have contact with the chairperson of the local Master Gardener group, and can put you in touch should you be thinking of joining. (The Master Gardener Program is a national volunteer organizations with numerous local chapters and is devoted to horticultural knowledge and practical application.) It's also a great way, he said, for newcomers to meet other newcomers as well as natives. "It's an opportunity to join up with people who have similar interests, to socialize and become a part of the community."

The Vidals go so far as to suggest that you might even want to consider turning a garden into a small business. If you're not feeling quite that ambitious, you can certainly take advantage of enjoying local produce in season — something that's harder to do back in the city. And think "local" in general. "Support local farmers," the Vidals advise, "even if the prices might not be the rock bottom you would pay by driving ten miles to a bulk importer store."

On the subject of food, the Vidals have a savvy tip if ever there was one: "If you want to begin to be accepted, grow something. Then ask for advice." In general, they suggest, "Be slow to give advice, but ask for plenty. And be thankful in following it." The genius of the Vidals' wisdom is this: By asking advice and being thankful when you get it, you honor the native. You're telling him or her, "You know something I don't, and I appreciate and respect you for that." As in so much of the wisdom folks are offering in this book, the common thread here is "respect." It's all about that old Aretha Franklin song: "R-E-S-P-E-C-T"—that's what both natives and newcomers are perhaps craving most. By practicing the wisdom of that song in your new environment, you'll build more cultural bridges than you can cross in a lifetime!

But if all those thorny, practical details of day-to-day country living pose a steep learning curve for you, one of the best sources of all-purpose information is the aforementioned *Grit* magazine. Touting itself as "America's Rural Lifestyle Magazine for 125 Years" (and counting), *Grit* is a fun read and a reliable guide on just about any practical aspect of living in the country. Earlier, you met the erudite Hank Will, *Grit's* country-seasoned editor and jack-of-all-trades, who told us that Grit "includes some do-it-yourself tips—how to build a barn, perhaps, or how to do some fencing. How to build a backyard barbeque. Anything that will help our readers enjoy their time out on the land."

A recent issue of *Grit* indeed had something for everyone. A machine and equipment nut, Hank Will himself reported on tests he'd done at his farm of new garden tiller and log-splitter models. There were articles on what to do with bored teenagers when you're a country Mom, on weed control, on aesthetically-pleasing rural mailboxes, on the best kinds of sheep-guard dogs, on how to start a backyard fruit orchard, and more. All presented in reader-friendly prose and with eye-friendly photographs and diagrams. It's a "feel good" magazine about a lifestyle you must be drawn to by moving here—but full of basic information that will make daily life go down a little more smoothly in your new home.

Another publication well worth a read is *Progressive Farmer,* "Serving Landowners Since 1886." Don't be fooled by the magazine's title: Although its approach is certainly "progressive," the target audience isn't just farmers, but any rural landowner. Subjects in a recent issue include a rural Indiana professional firefighter who grows 30,000 chili pepper plants on the side, an old one-room schoolhouse preserved by a landowner in Oklahoma, and the decline in bobwhite quail and whipporwill populations due primarily to habitat loss (for you bird-lovers, that's a land-use issue joined at the hip with farmland loss). Like *Grit,* this Birmingham, Alabama-based monthly is great brain food for your country life.

One more thing you'll want to consider is either joining the Virginia Farm Bureau or at least keeping abreast of its multi-faceted rural Virginia programs and activities. The Virginia Farm Bureau Federation has its finger on the pulse of the rural scene as well as anyone—maybe better than anyone—and it's been around a long time. An informative book by

The Virginia Farm Bureau and its board members are an **unsurpassed resource** for anything you may want to know about how farming is practiced in your county.

J. Hiram Ziglar of Weyers Cave, in Augusta County—*The Virginia Farm Bureau Story: Growth of a Grassroots Organization*—chronicles the history of the Virginia Farm Bureau from its origins in cooperative farm supply systems that aimed to lower farmers' costs. Since the Rockingham (County) Cooperative Farm Bureau was organized in 1921, later to become part of the Virginia Farm Bureau Federation, the Virginia Farm Bureau has fought tooth-and-nail for farm and rural life preservation, always mindful of the umbilical cord between land preservation and the financial sustainability of farming. Its impact on Virginia public and political awareness of the importance of farming has been second to none.

Even if you don't become a member, stop by the county Farm Bureau office and get to know some of the office folks. They'll have their ears to the ground for current vibrations from all the rural corners of the county. Find out who the county Farm Bureau board members are—typically they're farmers, like Corky Shackleford and Carl Tinder—and together they comprise an unsurpassed resource for anything you may want to know about how farming is practiced in your county. Invariably, they're down-to-earth, civic-minded people, deeply vested in the community, and—assuming they're not in the thick of harvesting or getting a crop to market!—talking with you will be a priority.

And while you're down at the Farm Bureau office, see if you can beg, borrow or steal the latest issue of *Virginia Farm Bureau News*, the monthly magazine. Find out what sheep shearing is all about in Tazewell County; why beekeeping has become more challenging, and how bee loss affects all of us; and why veteran observers of agriculture at Farm Bureau believe balancing locally grown food with agriculture's overall needs is our best guarantor of a reliable food supply. It's a good magazine; its subtext, always, is what we need to do to continue to have good food.

Good food—good life. All in all, it is a good life—no, a *great* life—out here in the country. The more things you know how to do, and the more you know about what's here for the doing, the greater you'll enjoy living this lifestyle. The same goes for the kids, if kids are a part of your equation. Though arguably there are more things "to do" in the city—a favorite critique of rural life by those infamously "bored" teens—country living is *engaged* living—active, not passive living. Life in the country requires you to do things yourself, to figure things out, to be challenged and stretched by an environment much bigger than the artificially-created, human-centric environment of cities.

So congratulate yourself. You're here because you dare to be. You trust yourself. You're not afraid to grow…and just like the life out here—that's a great thing!

O kay, it's not utopia, is it? A great life, but not utopia — believe we mentioned that fact, some time back.

There are things going on here that just irritate the heck out of you. And you know what? That's to be expected. As much as we've tried to make the case that farmers aren't folks to be "put out to pasture," it's also true that living where farmers live isn't always a bowl of cherries.

Land. From the earliest days of this country, land has always been big. *Very* big. So big, you just can't mess with it. No matter the amount of acreage, land is the ultimate entitlement — own land, and what's a neighbor going to do if he doesn't cotton to some of your ways? Every effort has been made, for centuries now, to protect the rights of that landowner.

So you have your land — you paid for it dearly — and your farmer neighbor has hers. That's the American way. But she does things that at least occasionally irritate you and because you're close to her — just right across the road — it's impossible to escape those things. You hear them. You smell them. Sometimes, you can't get around them with your car and sometimes you wonder why *her* needs trump yours…what's fair about that?

Well, there's that primacy of land ownership. But what about zoning, you ask? What about land use restrictions?

True enough, those laws pertaining to land often do challenge that primacy. But in this case—no. And there's a reason for that. Because, hand-in-glove with the farmer's needs is society's need to avoid starvation. Your neighbor is a farmer. She gets food to people. She has been granted a legal right to get her job done.

Across the United States, many states and localities have implemented "Right-To-Farm" laws aimed to ensure that farmers keep getting that food to your table. In Virginia, agriculture is the state's leading industry, so for economic reasons it makes plain common sense to protect a farmer's right to farm. Too much is at stake for society not to do that.

Virginia's "Right to Farm Law," when you try to read it, is the English language so abused only a politician could find pleasure in it. Essentially what you need to know is this—counties must legally protect a farmer's ability to produce food in an area zoned for agriculture, and they can't cook up zoning ordinances that "unreasonably restrict or regulate farm structures or farming and forestry practice."

As a practical matter, Virginia's Farm Law makes it extremely difficult to shut down or alter the character of a farm based on what some newcomers might think of as a public nuisance. "No agricultural operation or any of its appurtenances shall be or become a nuisance, private or public, if such operations are conducted in accordance with existing best management practices and comply with existing laws and regulations of the Commonwealth. The provisions of this section shall not apply whenever a nuisance results from the negligent or improper operation of any such agricultural operation or its appurtenances."

Got that? It means that the smell wafting your way from across the road isn't going away any time soon.

Which isn't to say that the farmer isn't being regulated to high heaven. He is. As you'd expect, quite a few of those regulations are as popular with farmers as making up snow days is with school kids. Wherever you travel, you'll find plenty of commotion among farmers about being regulated. Shawn Crocker, executive director of the Florida Strawberry Growers Association in Plant City, Florida, is quoted in a recent The Grower magazine article as saying, "We're regulating ourselves out of business." Crocker claims to have counted "forty-three local, regional, state and federal agencies that regulate the farming industry."

We don't doubt that figure. Every farmer deals with an overload of regulations—whether it's with how much, and at what times, pesticides can be applied to their crops, or worker's rights of much-needed immigrant labor. Where

Crocker seems a bit of a "squawker" is in his contention that regulations are driving farming itself out of business. Regulations—let's be frank—are often a necessary evil. Protecting consumers is important and is nothing to fool around with. Too frequently, regulations have been used conveniently as a straw man—railed against as the root of all agricultural misery when in fact there are other, and much larger, looming menaces to the future of farming.

But for you, the bottom line here is: as long as your neighbor across the road is farming by the rules, that's pretty much all she wrote. End of story...Unless the rules change.

What this all means is that it's a good idea to find out just when the earthy scent of manure applications will likely be wafting your way (Ask your neighbor. If you're on his side, he'll be glad to tell you; if you are really lucky, he may give you some for your lawn). Or when a farmer will be applying pesticides to crops (spring to late summer, but again, ask). Or when the roads are most likely to boast farm vehicles and maybe a thick cloud of dust. This list goes on. Knowing ahead of time will allow you to make any adjustments you deem appropriate—including scheduling that getaway to Acapulco!

Encouragingly, efforts to educate newcomers about farming may frequently be paying off. Not long ago, Ottawa County in Michigan produced a brochure for newcomers that included a small panel on which people could scratch and sniff an accurate whiff of cow manure. To the delight of the brochure's designers, odor complaints in Ottawa County dropped the year of the brochure's release to zero. Newcomers got the two basic points. Point one: No whining. Point two: Manure happens.

For what it's worth: We have never met a gardener or farmer who does not love the smell of well-rotted cow manure.

SAVING FARMLAND: your role

There may well be "fifty ways to leave your lover," according to singer Paul Simon—or was it sixty?—we're having a senior moment. But, unfortunately, there seem to be quite a few less ways to save farmland. The most direct way, of course, is for farmers to do it themselves. But that's a bit like asking your dog to find his meals on his own. Maybe he could do it; never underestimate the resourcefulness of a dog. But you're hardly increasing the chances of canine survival.

Recognizing that farmers need help—and that saving farmers money helps save farmland—Virginia government has stepped in to exempt farmers from paying taxes on a wide variety of farm-related items. The list reads like a twenty-fifth century archeologist's inventory of a twenty-first century farm "dig": farm machinery, tools, equipment, repair parts, fruit and vegetable containers, baler twine—the list goes on around the barn, and it includes items for which that archeologist might only, if she's lucky, find bones: llamas, turkey poults, rabbits. You get the idea: don't tax the farmer straight into the hay baler. He might get chewed up.

In 2001, Virginia also created the Office of Farmland Preservation. The agency is a central clearinghouse for preservation, developing preservation strategies and policies (such as those applying to easements on farmland) while at the same time co-ordinating local efforts and the efforts of established organizations like the America Farmland Trust. Additionally, the Office conducts educational programs on preservation, provides technical assistance to farmers, and—through the Virginia Farm Link program it manages—connects retiring farmers with active or aspiring farmers. When that linkage works, happily the farm's transition is not to a new tract house development, but to a new farmer working on that land.

One state agency deserving special note is the Virginia Outdoors Foundation, which makes itself available to any landowner wanting to throw the brakes on "progress." Essentially, in exchange for restrictions on property development—restrictions that then become a permanent part of any deed transfer—the Outdoors Foundation becomes a conduit for significant tax breaks on the property. Landowners must weigh the impact of those restrictions—which do, in fact, allow limited development—on the potential sales value of their land, over and against the positives of permanent, irrevocable land or farm preservation.

So critical is this issue of farmland loss that most everywhere you travel in America these days, state and county governments are looking at any additional ideas—no matter how seemingly problematic—that could conceivably help preserve farmland. One of those ideas—a concept called "transferable development rights"—has surfaced and been successfully applied in an unlikely place: Montgomery County, Maryland, which borders Washington, D.C., and which—as Dr. Royce Hanson told us—"is one of the most robustly growing metropolitan areas in the country."

Remarkably, in a county sitting elbow-to-elbow with an urban giant, almost 100,000 acres in Montgomery County have been permanently preserved since 1980 in what Dr. Royce described as "an agricultural reserve." That's nearly one-third of Montgomery County, a huge swath of land along the northern and western edges of the county devoted to farms and forests, and in which, by all accounts, farmers are thriving. How could such a thing be possible so close to Washington?

To learn how, we sat down with Dr. Hanson in his office in Silver Spring. Though retired from the political science department at American University and seemingly in his 70s, Dr. Hanson on the day we met him was all energy and animation, en route from our meeting with him to an evening board meeting after a day that started in his office at 7 A.M. He walked briskly, talked briskly, hewed closely to the point—this "doer" who grew up doing chores on a northwestern Arkansas farm, the man widely given the most credit for what some have called "the Montgomery County Miracle." Though the concept of transferable development rights (or TDR) was not new—it was first applied in New York City—it was Dr. Hanson who first applied TDR to farmland, and who first conceived the idea, as he put it, "of transferring rights from one location to another location some distance away."

"Property," Dr. Hanson explained to us in his gravelly voice, "is basically a bundle of rights. You have the right of access, the right of possession, the right to use. One of the rights to use is the right to develop your land. Transferring development rights is the idea that the *right* to develop can be severed from the land itself. And you can sell that right to someone else who needs it to increase the amount of development that they can do on their land. So in the agricultural preserve, the land had been zoned at one unit per five acres. We were downsizing it to one unit for twenty-five acres, as the maximum amount of development that could occur. And as we did that, we said to the farmers, 'All right, since we're down-zoning your land, you can retain one development right for each five acres. And then in other parts of the county where we have public facilities that are sufficient to support local density, owners of land there can buy your development rights, and they can build one more unit of housing for every development right that they buy from you.' Basically, we created a private market that made it possible to protect land. Because when a farmer sells his development rights to a builder, he also places an easement in perpetuity that says, 'I've given up the right to build so many houses on this land forever. Every time the farm changes hands, that easement stays with it. And in the meantime the farmer has gained some income, because one of the big issues we confronted when we were working this out in the late 70s was that farmers—particularly small farmers—have a lot of their family fortune tied up in the land. That's their equity, that's their retirement. So being able to sell their rights, and keep, spend, or invest the money, protected that element of their equity."

You, too, can help in preserving farmland.

Supporting your local farmer by buying his products—that should certainly be at or near the top of your list. Supporting the adoption of farmer-friendly preservation ordinances—that's a key, too.

Montgomery County's success story has become a model for some governments looking to save farmland—in Chatham County, North Carolina, and elsewhere—but Dr. Hanson is the first to concede that the TDR approach isn't for everyone. "One of the key things you need to make it work," he explained, "is a strong market for housing in the area. The development rights have to be worth something to somebody. Because the market for building here has traditionally been so strong, it was possible to create this market. So, in our situation, the developers got on board, and ultimately a good number of the farmers came on board with it as well. In fact, some of the people who were very skeptical of the program initially have become strong advocates of it. I think now that while some people in the agricultural community still want to cash out, there's a strong feeling across the whole rural community that the reserve is a very important asset. It provides an opportunity for farming to continue."

That farming continues to exist in Montgomery County is a clear benefit of the TDR approach. But Dr. Hanson also enumerated several less obvious reasons why saving farmland benefits the entire region. "One of the critical problems of major metropolitan areas," he said, "is having areas that are large enough to provide a big carbon sink, if you will, for an area. Well, agricultural land does that. A lot of this land is also forested, so it provides enormous environmental benefits in the form of improved air and water quality. Now, most of our farmers are really "best practices" farmers, using techniques in cropping that are environmentally sensitive. And because all of this area drains into the Chesapeake Bay, the Chesapeake Bay Foundation has been a very strong supporter of the reserve."

"Another very important aspect," Dr. Hansen continues, "is economic. Agriculture is one of the top-grossing industries in this county, providing a substantial annual product. Another benefit is cultural—agriculture helps a community retain its rural character, and there's a historic consciousness in that. A unique kind of contribution is made to the overall culture of the county when you maintain a rural area within a large, urbanizing community."

Inspiring as it is as a model of what government can accomplish, Montgomery County's story needn't make you think that individual efforts aren't significant. As someone perhaps new to rural Virginia, you, too, can help in preserving farmland. Supporting your local farmer by buying his products—that should certainly be at or near the top of your list. Supporting the adoption of farmer-friendly preservation ordinances—that's a key, too. But you can also make plans to enroll your property in a land trust, a concept of easement-granting similar to the agreement you would make with the Virginia Outdoors Foundation, and another effective tool in preserving rural land. Or, perhaps, you might even to try to sell some or much of your property to a farmer—a financial sacrifice, certainly, but also, in every sense, a sacrifice for the good of the country. If that's a bit too altruistic for you, then at least consider making yourself available for volunteering with farmland educational programs, or supporting—with your dollars—organizations like American Farmland Trust.

Though it's not high on the media's—or politicians'—list of priorities, the threat to the future of the Nation from farmland loss is very real and increasingly urgent. We hope you'll join farmers themselves, and many others, in this important work.

THOSE
SURPRISING
{ sometimes }
EASEMENTS

When easements and rural land mix (we don't mean conservation easements), one of two things — without a lawyer — is bound to happen: **a)** Neither you nor any other interested party will have the foggiest idea what's going on; or, **b)** you and the other party will have a foggy idea — and then go at each other's throats in the fog.

T hrow a lawyer or two into the mix and it's anyone's guess what will happen. That's because easements — after first catching people by surprise — seem to break half the rules of the sanctity of private property. So what sort of critter are we talking about here? Well, the definition we like best of the sort of easement in question is, "a property interest that allows the holder of the easement to use property that he or she does not possess."

Sounds un-American, but it isn't — and for good reason. Easements address that problem many of us have had at one time another: the problem of access. In this case, access to property we own that can only be "gotten to" through someone else's property. Inherently, that's a ticklish situation — and to prevent fisticuffs, the mighty arm of the law has to reach in. But because the situations the laws address are sometimes complicated, it's worth a moment to try to figure the basics out.

Let's say you've moved into a rural area and are buying property some distance off a public road. Happens all the time. What you want to be sure of is that there's clear title to an easement across someone else's property — that nothing's ambiguous about your right to get to your place — nor about the width of the road through the other person's land or who can use that road. At the same time, if someone holds an easement on *your* property, you want to make sure that only that person accesses your land, unless you grant that right to others. Possessing an easement does not allow the easement holder to occupy the land, or to keep others off that land unless they interfere with the easement holder's use. As the landowner, you, however, can continue to use the easement — unimpeded by anyone — and at the same time have the right to exclude anyone else except the easement holder.

We know of a case in rural Floyd County in which an easement holder believed that he had *carte blanche* to invite anyone he wished to use his easement to access his property. What he had in mind, specifically, were city friends who wanted to hunt deer. So one deer season, the friends came in droves, using the easement road as the landowner's simmering anger boiled into rage. Finally, the landowner confronted the easement holder — a second-homer who only occasionally came out to his property, even as his buddies blasted away with their rifles for the duration of deer season. Ultimately, both landowner and easement holder hired attorneys, and the easement holder learned that only he — not half of Roanoke — could use the easement unless granted permission.

When misunderstandings like this one arise, what's written in the deed is critical. Deed descriptions of easements can vary widely, contingent on agreements that may have been hammered out a hundred — or five — years ago. What's critical, also, is establishing at the outset an understanding about usage between the easement holder and the landowner. Don't wait until someone's become accustomed to abusing the terms of the easement; it may be too late, then, to set that person straight — short of hiring an attorney. Have a talk early, and try to establish trust. In real life, things often boil down to that personal relationship, to trust or the lack of it. And without that trust, seemingly small abuses of the easement stipulations begin to loom large — and lead to conflict.

One other basic thing you should know. The *Code of Virginia* states: "Owners of forest and timberlands may obstruct or close private and seldom used roadways." It's a misdemeanor to "destroy, remove, or leave the obstruction unlocked or open." Though there's ambiguity about what "seldom used" may mean, part of the idea here is to protect a landowner from the nuisance of intrusions onto her property made more likely by an absentee easement holder who rarely accesses his property. "Forests and timberlands" — which could potentially be logged in this situation — play a role, too. Theoretically, keeping that gate closed discourages intruders from making merry smack dab in the middle of a logging operation.

Under this law, an easement holder, "upon making use of the roadway," is required to keep the gate or chain locked behind them. If this applies to you — don't lose your key!

GOOD FENCES MAKE GOOD NEIGHBORS

We admire how Dr. Leon Geyer, Professor of Agricultural Law at Virginia Tech, introduced the topic of Virginia fence law several years back: *"Fence law and its application are often the subject of neighborly disagreement."* That's certainly a gentlemanly way of putting it. In our experience, what Dr. Geyer discreetly did not go on to say was this: "They are also, sometimes, the subject of distinctly *unneighborly* disagreement."

This topic has your name written on it more than you may think. Fences — and boundary line friction — are ubiquitous in rural Virginia, and your chances of avoiding a "fence moment" are not always great. Take this scenario: The division fence between you and a neighbor is in sore need of replacement. Repair attempts have failed to control your neighbor's rambunctious cows, and you've concluded, enough is enough, and want to build a new fence. But who pays for it? A law revised in 2005 says that if you're a homeowner (or various other things, but are not a livestock farmer), you aren't required to help pay for that fence. The revised law nullifies the prior requirement that you pay half the cost of the fence.

In other situations, however, it may be worth your while to co-pay. In general, division fences that establish clear boundary lines are a good idea. When no division fence has been built, the law says that "either one of the adjoining owners may give notice in writing of his desire and intention to build such a fence to the owner of the adjoining land, or to his agent, and require him to come forward and build his half thereof." When this notice has been received, the adjoining landowner has ten days to give notice of his intention to let his land lie open, in which case he has no obligation to co-pay for the fence. If, however, he gives no notice, and if, after thirty days, he takes no action to help build the fence, he's liable for half the cost.

However this all plays out, once the fence is up it's legally deemed a

division fence. And for all practical purposes, that fence will be regarded as the boundary line. So it's important, as a landowner, that you get involved early in the game—and make sure that the fence really is following the surveyed boundary line. In many cases, it's a good idea to have the line "run"—i.e., a new survey done, just to be sure the fence is going up where it should be going up.

When you read Robert Frost's poem "Mending Wall," you realize that the idea that "Good fences make good neighbors" is only part of the poem's thesis. What the poem also suggests [Consider the: "Why do they make good neighbors?"] is that it's always important to try to cooperate with your neighbor, and that's certainly the right idea here. The best case scenario will see cooperation from the start, and—when appropriate—each neighbor paying half. The enduring good will between neighbors will be well worth the price of a division fence.

"Mending Wall"

Something there is that doesn't love a wall,
That sends the frozen-ground-swell under it,
And spills the upper boulders in the sun;
And makes gaps even two can pass abreast.
The work of hunters is another thing:
I have come after them and made repair
Where they have left not one stone on stone,
But they would have the rabbit out of hiding,
To please the yelping dogs. The gaps I mean,
No one has seen them made or heard them made,
But at spring mending-time we find them there.
I let my neighbor know beyond the hill;
And on a day we meet to walk the line
And set the wall between us once again.
We keep the wall between us as we go.
To each the boulders that have fallen to each.
And some are loaves and some so nearly balls
We have to use a spell to make them balance:
"Stay where you are until our backs are turned!"
We wear our fingers rough with handling them.
Oh, just another kind of outdoor game,
One on a side. It comes to little more:
He is all pine and I am apple-orchard.
My apple trees will never get across
And eat the cones under his pines, I tell him.
He only says, "Good fences make good neighbors."
Spring is the mischief in me, and I wonder
If I could put a notion in his head:
"Why do they make good neighbors? Isn't it
Where there are cows? But here there are no cows.
Before I built a wall I'd ask to know
What I was walling in or walling out,
And to whom I was like to give offence.
Something there is that doesn't love a wall,
That wants it down!" I could say "Elves" to him,
But it's not elves exactly, and I'd rather
He said it for himself. I see him there,
Bringing a stone grasped firmly by the top
In each hand, like an old-stone savage armed.
He moves in darkness as it seems to me,
Not of woods only and the shade of trees.
He will not go behind his father's saying,
And he likes having thought of it so well
He says again, "Good fences make good neighbors."

— **Robert Frost**
from *North of Boston* (1915)

VIRGINIA'S ANIMAL KINGDOM and you

Should another universal flood come our way—and Noah be called out of retirement—he'd have his hands full rounding up two of every animal in rural Virginia.

All manner of commercial livestock live here, of course, including critters like alpacas introduced by enterprising farmers. Then there are the wild animals—now including coyotes—a real menagerie in the sense that almost all the wild animals are pretty much on display, living as they do in such proximity to humans. Certainly it's a rare week when you won't catch sight of deer in rural Virginia. That Carroll County bear that came calling one recent spring on a beekeeper's hives was not as astounding a sight as one might think. The bear had business to attend to in territory only theoretically zoned for humans—and no doubt will be heard from again.

When it comes to livestock, farmers can be, understandably, a little touchy. Though their nocturnal serenades may call us romantically to the wild, marauding coyotes will win few votes among farmers. Even that bear, in all its majestic beauty, will have a hard time making friends with the beekeeper, or with the orchardist whose cherry blossoms rely on honeybees for pollination.

Touchy as they can be about animals, farmers can be equally touchy about animal-loving newcomers. Call it "the Bambi factor," call it that understandable affection urban folks have for animals—there's often a culture gap when farmers and newcomers talk about the same critters. Whether it's with deer—or that beef cow that a newcomer might think is starving or sick—we've seen, time and again, that "East is East, and West is West, and never the twain shall meet," as Rudyard Kipling put it. Truth be told, it's one of the sorest points between the two cultures.

Essentially, for farmers, there are two categories of things to "beef" about here: First, their livestock is, after all, *their* livestock. Second, the question of what to do about that deer population, or even that "cute" bear that did, after all, cause significant damage to expensive beehives and jeopardized a cherry crop.

The livestock issue has several facets. One has to do with something that would almost seem laughable—except that, in a worst-case scenario, it wouldn't be at all funny. Domesticated animals can be large and ornery. They can also be, in certain situations, dangerous. Farmers observing newcomers on their property who seem oblivious to the danger can become just a wee bit stressed. As delightful as it can be to see a child (or adult) admiring an outstanding animal, farmers want newcomers to know that, alas, their farm isn't a petting zoo. It wasn't set up for that. The same farmer who worries every day about farm safety with tractors and farm equipment will also be concerned about the safety of anyone else on her property. Additionally, farmers know that people can spread diseases to animals; while that's not the issue of greatest concern, it can be on a farmer's mind. The bottom line with both these concerns: **Ask a farmer before you approach her animals.**

A second livestock issue surfaces with what may seem to be surprising frequency. A number of farmers, including Rob Harrison, who runs a cow-calf operation in central Virginia, have related to us what amounts to the same story. Driving down the road, a newcomer spots a cow or cows that to the newcomer's untrained eye look like they are "starving." Maybe she doesn't see hay. Maybe she never ran cattle for a living. The newcomer then calls the animal control folks, rather than the farmer who owns the cows. As Rob Harrison tells this story, the next thing he sees—when he arrives home—is a sheriff's department or animal control car in his yard.

"Newcomers," one farmer told us, "often feel a claim to being an off-site manager. 'That fence needs to be fixed,' they'll say. Or whatever. They've got to be commenting on your management. Unfortunately—like with cows 'starving'—they don't call the owner. They call the sheriff or animal control."

An obvious lesson from what you've just read: *if something seems amiss on a farm, talk with the farmer directly.* Sometimes, in fact, something really is amiss—and if your intention is to be helpful, a farmer will be grateful to you, especially if he didn't know about it. Occasionally, for sure, a fence really is broken, and a farmer wasn't aware of it. Which may lead, say, to cows standing in the middle of the road. In a situation like this, Rob Harrison offers this advice: "People need to understand that animals standing in the road don't know what's going on. Slow down!"

And once you slow down—what do you do about those cows on the loose?

Well, never assume that the farmer knows his cows are out of the pasture—call him. He'll appreciate it. If you aren't sure who owns the cows, then call a neighbor who might know.

A third livestock issue has to do with dogs. If you own a dog, and your dog acts aggressively with someone else's livestock, there are consequences. The *Code of Virginia* provides compensation under certain conditions for livestock ($400 maximum) and poultry ($10 maximum) killed by dogs. In addition, animal control or other officers are authorized to kill a dog in the act of killing, injuring, or harassing livestock or poultry.

When the subject shifts to wild animals, clearly, farmers have no jurisdiction here...right? Here, farmers and newcomers alike must defer to the rights of wild animals not to be driven from their habitat—to be treated deferentially.

Well, let's dig a little deeper. Farmers—like most other native rural landowners—have had their share of exposure to wild animals. So the glasses are a few shades shy of being rose-colored. If you're an orchardist, you've known since you were a kid that those furry, cuddly groundhogs can girdle the trunk of a young apple tree your dad just set out last spring—and kill it. If you raise goats, you're keenly aware that behind that primordial coyote's howl in the middle of the night is a very sharp set of teeth. If you're any kind of rural landowner, you know that deer populations have exploded in Virginia, leading to a host of environmental problems, not to mention problems for agriculture.

Add to these realities the traditional love of hunting in rural Virginia; stir in many a newcomer's aversion to guns and hunting—and, when it comes to wild animals, you have a volatile mix.

What natives hope newcomers will understand is that—while hunting may be a sport, and, for many folks, a tradition that runs back in the family for many generations—it's also, these days, often serving a useful purpose. Nothing could better underscore that point than deer-hunting. It used to be true—and still is, to some extent—that venison appeared regularly on rural dinner tables, a cheap and healthful dietary staple. But with deer now overrunning the countryside, reducing deer population by hunting is doing everyone a big favor—including, arguably, Bambi's cousins themselves, doing their doe-eyed best to wreak havoc on the ecosystems that sustain them.

This point is not lost on folks with whom we talked. Ralph Yowell of Madison County takes it a step further in this advice to newcomers: "Do your part to control wildlife populations by allowing some legal hunting on your property." Newcomers Dean and Susan Vidal elaborate on Yowell's point: "Consider allowing neighbors to hunt on your land, whether you are a gun advocate or not. Our state is overrun with deer, as you can see along the road. Hunters provide a useful service in thinning overpopulation. "

Good ideas here. But if the thought of camouflaged hunters tramping your property just gives you the heebie-jeebies, take the time to get acquainted with neighbors steeped in the customs and culture of hunting. You may be surprised. We know of one woman who moved from Los Angeles to a rural Virginia county who did just that—and was pleasantly surprised that none of her stereotypes were confirmed. In fact, she found her deer hunting neighbors to be solicitous and gentlemanly, and she ate up their colorful hunting stories. In exchange for the use of her land, she got on the venison gravy train, stocking her freezer with it every year. She even learned how to make venison sausage in a way that even a Martha Stewart would envy—seasoning it with bourbon and cranberries.

If you do grant hunters the right to hunt on your property, you'll definitely need to know in advance just when they'll be there, and what the shooting rules are with respect to your whereabouts and those of family members. And you'll want 100% compliance with the rules you lay down—anything short of that is a breach of trust that will, necessarily, cause you to terminate hunting privileges.

One potential problem for newcomers who buy is the "succession" problem. As Lucius Bracey, a Charlottesville-based attorney who owns rural property reminded us, "At times, former landowners think they still own the land. They think they still have hunting rights." Situations of this sort can put the diplomatic skills of any newcomer to a stern test, as one Patrick County newcomer told us who did not want hunting of any sort—period—on her newly acquired Blue Ridge Mountain property. When the former landowner approached her to ask if he could continue deer-hunting there, "I overreacted a little bit," she told us. "I told him it was nothing personal, but I just don't like people killing wild animals." Though she never relented, later she realized her words and tone caused offense, and in the years since the encounter she's made every effort to be kind to the man and his family, allowing them to walk freely on her land and always bringing Christmas presents. "Without coming across as weak," she told us, "I should have been more sympathetic at the start to the genuine loss he felt when he could no longer hunt here. For him, it was like losing an old friend."

We can't allow the subject of deer-hunting to pass without flagging a problem that seems, if anything, to be getting worse every year: outright poaching. Many hunters, as Corky Shackleford reminded us, are not farmers or even rural landowners; yet the vast majority are true sportsmen, far more enjoying the outdoor experience, the stalking, the quiet, than the harvest.

In dramatic contrast to these sportsmen are the poachers. We know of a number of instances in which—unbeknownst at first to the landowner—deer poachers have stolen onto private land and taken deer under cover of darkness, spotlighting deer with vehicle headlights and then blasting away. Other poachers operate in broad daylight, such as the two

Poachers on private property are held in utter contempt by true sportsmen; so it follows that sportsmen are the natural allies of the landowner.

poachers a Carroll County farmer encountered on his land one Thanksgiving morning several years ago. That farmer is probably fortunate to be alive; he was working that morning in a field when he spotted two strangers with rifles sidling into the woods at the edge of his field. When they refused to answer him, he charged after them, unarmed and cursing. Moments later a concealed pickup burst out of the woods and raced past him *en route* to a county road. Later that day, relating the incident to his family at Thanksgiving dinner, he counted himself lucky not to have been shot.

With understaffed game wardens often miles away or swamped with calls, problems of this sort—problems that for men can escalate into testosterone-laden showdowns—can be hard to solve. Perhaps the best advice we can give a new landowner—if it's possible in a moment of fury—is to not echo the farmer's outraged curses. Try to stay cool, to speak calmly (if firmly) to the poacher, to get a license plate number if possible. If it's your desire, make sure, of course, that your land is posted, and don't hesitate to report the incident to the game warden. Needless to say, don't even daydream about doing some poaching. The skin you save may be your own.

One last thing you should know. Under Virginia law, farmers whose fruit trees, crops, livestock, or personal property are being damaged by deer or bear can report the damage to authorities who, in turn, when they confirm the damage, can authorize the farmer to kill the offending animals. In the case of bears, authorities have the option to capture and relocate them, an option frequently exercised. There are limits—authorities typically will specify how many animals can be killed, the duration for which authorization applies, the hours when killing can and can't occur, and the shooting zone relative to residential areas.

RULES OF THE ROAD

Let's join Willie Nelson and get "on the road again"—first, with a deer. This will be our last word about wild animals—and it's a word for the wise. Don't let deer become roadkill. **Better yet, don't let yourself become roadkill.**

Increasingly on rural highways, deer and vehicles are having close encounters—too close. So drive cautiously, especially after dark; if you do see a deer at the side of the road—and if it's safe to do so vis-à-vis other traffic—stop your vehicle and wait for the deer to figure out its next move. One farmer we know saw a deer on the side of a rural road and kept driving toward it, albeit slowly. At the very last moment—naturally—the deer bolted straight onto the road and plowed across the hood of the farmer's car. The results weren't pretty: the deer hobbled into the darkness of the woods, who knows whether to live or die, and the eight-year-old car was declared a total loss.

As Charlottesville-area farmer Steve Murray pointed out to us, the unfortunate proximity of deer to vehicles in transit is yet another argument for controlling deer population. Said Steve, wryly summing it up for the upscale newcomers among us: "That BMW is expensive to fix."

Meanwhile, there may be a lesson here for folks following farm vehicles on rural roads: Patience, with a capital "P." Neither the lack of patience evident in the driver's reluctance to stop his car, nor sudden moves—like that of the deer—come to a good end. Remember that BMW driver and farmer on his tractor we mentioned some time back? On that curvy road? In that case, the trailing BMW driver impatiently sat on his horn, infuriating the tractor-driver, who, with no way to pull over, continued down the road. Luckily, no accident ensued. But across rural roads in Virginia, accidents *are* occurring, often from lack of patience. A tractor-driver employed by cattle farmer Rob Harrison—attempting a left-hand turn—was rear-ended by the impatient driver of a car, injuring Harrison's employee. And, as Harrison told us matter-of-factly, "You can't drive a tractor down a road without being cursed at."

This subject prompted a recent *Virginia Farm Bureau News* article on the subject featuring Dinwiddie County farmer Dale Martin. Newcomers, Martin said, "are moving in and don't really understand…They don't realize that this equipment is big and they need to slow down." The article quoted Virginia State Trooper John L. Lewis. Speaking of newcomer road rage, Trooper Lewis remarked dryly: "The hand signals you're seeing are not the ones for turning right or left."

Yup—we got that. But instead of inviting farmers on rural roads to—well, you know as well as we do what those "hand signals" mean—why not be civil and make the best of an inherently frustrating situation? Look carefully the next time you come upon wide farm equipment; quite often the tractor driver has no way to pull off and allow a driver to pass him.

When sharing the road with farm equipment, *Virginia Farm Bureau News* offered drivers four tips we quote verbatim:

1 Slow down to the speed of the vehicle as soon as you see a slow-moving vehicle emblem.

2 Watch for hand signals, and determine whether the equipment operator is preparing to turn.

3 Pass slowly and deliberately, watching for other traffic and sudden turns. Don't pull back into the travel lane too quickly.

4 Never pass farm equipment in a no-passing zone.

To these we'll add this "last but not least" fifth tip: —

5 As you get around the farmer and his farm equipment, flash him a big smile, give him a thumbs-up with your free hand, and, for good measure—if he's a man and you're a single woman—call cheerfully out the window and ask him if he's single. Oh, go ahead— we dare you.

COUNTRY WATER

The water out here in the country — It tastes good! — a lot of folks say that.

That said, it's often going to be up to you to pipe it to your lips. Urban water systems don't know their way around out here, though it is true that county-maintained community water systems can sometimes be found in rural counties. But don't count on it. Count, instead, if you're building a house, on digging a well to go with it. Or if you're buying a house, on making sure the existing well passes muster. Either way, it can be costly, and you'll need to have the water tested.

There are still native folks who pipe water in from a spring. If that is an option, don't rule it out—but before you go to the trouble of building tanks to store the water and laying the pipe, be sure to have the spring water tested. Odds are, coming out of a pristine place in the woods, it will taste very, very good—we know that from long experience. But be prepared to shell out the bigger bucks for well-digging, if needed.

If you're thinking of creating a dam for a pond, depending on its size and purpose you may need to get a construction permit from the Virginia Soil and Water Conservation Board, which involves classification of the dam based on its size and potential hazard to human life. You may also be required to work with an engineer. Ponds and dams have unique challenges to contend with, including dams giving way and folks downstream getting an unsolicited bath. Additionally, Virginia law requires that "no person may engage in any land-disturbing activity until he has submitted to the district or locality an erosion and sediment control plan for the land-disturbing activity and the plan has been reviewed and approved by the plan-approving authority." In other words, this isn't just ponds and dams we're talking about. Keep in mind that you can't just be a lone wolf and start shoving around big chunks of earth for whatever project you have in mind.

One of the hot-button environmental topics of recent years has been wetlands—how critical they are to the health of larger ecosystems, and how they're being used by human beings. It's possible you'll have wetlands on your property, particularly given the fine shadings of definitions of wetlands these days, such as "vegetatated" and "nonvegetated" wetlands. Taken as a whole, the

Code of Virginia defines wetlands as "an area that is inundated or saturated by surface or ground water at a frequency or duration sufficient to support, and that under normal conditions does support, a prevalence of vegetation typically adapted for life in saturated soil conditions, and that is subject to a perpetual easement permitting inundation by water."

Translation: If there's standing water on your property—or if you always sink knee deep into the ground there—and if plants are growing in that muck—then it may very well be wetlands by some definition. Which means it may be subject to easements or other protective measures, which will affect your unrestricted freedom to suck it dry or whatever other scheme you may have up your sleeve. Learn before you leap—find out what laws may apply to your situation, and proceed (cautiously) from there.

A creek or river running through or adjoining your property may trigger some of the same constraints. There are a variety of laws and accepted practices about what can and cannot be done with land next to streams—laws having to do with the potential for chemical or waste runoff, with soil erosion, with creations of buffers. In the old days, landowners could just "Let 'er rip"—fill those pristine streams with the *effluent du jour*—but that's no longer cool. What is cool is taking good care of our waterways—without shutting down business operations—and farmer or not, you'll need to know the rules in your locality.

Since water quality keeps us alive, what's good for the goose here is good for the gander. Take care of our water, take care of ourselves. Living back in the city, you may not have had to address that fact of life directly. Now, perhaps, you do. It may make you feel—well—a little more alive.

Green fields are beautiful; a green forest comes only from rain. Country folks know that raindrops are free silver dollars falling from the sky. Don't believe it? Try farming (or living, even) where "It don't."

You can tell where someone is "from" or how she thinks by listening to her appreciation for rain.

CITY GAL: "What a dreary day,"… "The sidewalks ruined my stockings,"… and "My dress shoes got soaked!"

COUNTRY GAL: "How much did you get?"… "The thunderstorm missed us, but Mary, next door, got an inch and a half!"…or "What a gullywasher!" (*said gratefully, but meaning: 'too much rain, too fast'*). "Lordy, we are dry; we could use a soaker."

HOMESITE
COMMON SENSE

One last topic to cover briefly before we return to relations with your neighbors: the site where you build your home.

We will keep this brief. We're sure everyone else you've talked to has weighed in with quite a litany of advice, and we know you have your own opinions. So your head's pretty full already. There are four words to keep in mind here: *Soil. Wind. Water. View.*

SOIL. Do you want to grow anything, or have livestock, on your property? If so, soil is a huge deal—get it tested. Talk to the County Extension agent about it. Compare your soil types to similar types in the neighborhood, and ask the owners of that land a million and one questions about their experience.

WIND. This is the one so often overlooked—and then it's too late. How much wind do you like? Does the number of windy days that occur, say, in Kansas, or on Cape Cod, appeal to you? Answer those questions, then examine the degree of exposure to wind at that site you're considering. Talk with your neighbors. Ask: How much wind do they get at similar sites? Are you a fairly typical human being—or an aspiring wind turbine? That's the question.

WATER. We've talked about water already, but what we didn't talk about is: How deep is the well-drilling likely to go? What's the quantity and quality of water on the property? And do any of your neighbors know, from experience, what happens to the water supply in dry weather?

VIEW. That's a word we've often used in the course of this book—and in a number of contexts. But now the question is, how does it mix with the wind factor? And how does it mix with how you feel when you see houses perched on top of ridgelines? ("Do unto others as…") How many trees are going to have to come down? Is higher always better, specifically on *your* property?

We promised we'd keep it brief. That's four words to think about—and twelve questions, count 'em—twelve—to answer. Once you've done all that—may you love your new home, and where you live.

CREATING
COMMUNITY

For our final topic, we want to return now to your relations with your new neighbors. But we want to put that discussion into a slightly different—and perhaps larger—context: creating community.

For that's what you're doing, by moving into rural Virginia, and being positive about living along-side your neighbors. You're creating community.

Community doesn't happen overnight. It takes time, resources and often, quite frankly, an attitude adjustment to start building the framework for a satisfying community life in the country. What's more, as the importance of community and connection becomes increasingly understood and accepted as a key ingredient in good health, making a concerted effort to engage in community life is one of the best investments you'll ever make.

Published in 2000, the book *Bowling Alone* by Robert Putnam, a professor of public policy at Harvard, is a landmark study of the importance of "social capital," defined by the author as "connections among individuals—social networks and the norms of reciprocity and trustworthiness that arise from them." Decrying what he believes to be a sharp decline in social capital in our society since 1970 or thereabouts, Putnam implores his readers: "Let us find ways to ensure that Americans will spend less time sitting passively alone in front of glowing screens and more time in active connection with our fellow citizens."

And he adds—significantly, for newcomers moving into a rural culture: "To build bridging social capital requires that we transcend our social and political and professional identities to connect with people unlike ourselves."

The follow-up book to *Bowling Alone* was *Better Together*, co-written by Putnam and researcher Louis Feldstein. We sat down with Feldstein in Boston, who told us that simple things people can do—bringing a meal to a friend, coaching in Little League, or hosting a dinner party—make a real, positive difference. "Americans are now invited to dinner parties eight times a year," Feldstein observed, "but in the mid-70's the average number of invitations was seventeen times a year." Feldstein thinks that we can do better than this, that we all benefit by spending more time connecting with each other.

"We know," Feldstein continued, "that in a community where social capital is higher—where there's more trust, more connectivity—people will likely be healthier. They will feel better about their life. Their schools will be better, their kids will be better educated. They will be safer, and their government will work better. That's powerful. If you had to choose whether you would spend more money in police on the streets or take the same amount of money and invest it in building social capital, choosing the latter would do more to make the neighborhood safe. If more people know who is on the street, and know their neighbors, the neighborhood will be safer."

The first—and last—thing you need to understand about rural life is that it's people-centered— far more so than in a city.

In rural America, people come first.

Perhaps most striking among Putnam's and Feldstein's conclusions is the effect social capital can have on personal health. "There is a huge amount of public health data," Feldstein told us, "incontrovertible—that connections make a huge difference. For example: If you are not a member of a single organization, and you join one organization, in that year your chances of dying drop fifty percent. If you join another organization that year, your chances of dying drop another twenty-five percent. Now, that flattens out. But the bottom line in this is that being alone is fatal. In fact, loneliness is as big a threat to your health as things like smoking or obesity. It is a close call as to which will kill you first, smoking three packs of cigarettes a day or being all alone. Literally."

The good news from Putnam's and Feldstein's research is that small towns and rural culture in general tend to have more social capital than most urban areas. In a sense, less is more here—people, who are here in smaller numbers, know and trust each other and are connected, which creates a great base from which newcomers can build even more social capital.

It follows, then, that the first—and last—thing you need to understand about rural life is that it's people-centered—far more so than in a city. In rural America, people come first. Although rural folks are generally more conservative politically and personally than city residents, due to the code of intense loyalty to "members of the family," enormous philosophical and political differences are tolerated once you are accepted into the fold. Kathleen Norris, author of the book Dakota, points to an old "bohemian radical" living in rural Lemmon, South Dakota, who used to work for a communist bookstore in California in the 1930s, who is now "one of the local characters, an irreplaceable old coot who we love and hate."

Because people who live in big cities generally know others by profession or occupation, their interpersonal dealings tend to be more stratified and often more limited. The actual experience of rural living is likely to thrust you into regular and personal contact with a far greater *range* of people of differing age groups, economic categories and educational levels. You might know the mayor of Staunton, a factory owner, and your auto mechanic equally well. And you're likely to encounter the *same* people time and again.

What's more, while in major metropolitan areas you may want to wad up and throw away someone with whom you've had a falling out, in the country, you're well advised to at least attempt to patch up differences. Someone offered this pearl of wisdom, and there's plenty of truth in it: "You don't hold grudges out in the country or in a small town."

When making a place for yourself in the country, you need to recognize that every community (no matter how small) has its own unique identity and culture that should be respected as that of a foreign land. Though rural residents sometimes get a bad rap for rigidity and intolerance, city critics let themselves off the hook when they move to a rural outpost and expect their behavior and individuality to be accepted—no matter how eccentric, alien, or off-putting—without understanding the local culture and putting forth an effort to adapt.

"You have to bend over backwards so people don't think you think you're better than they are," Mike Goldwasser told us, a one-time law student at the University of Pennsylvania who runs a cattle farm in Carroll County. Mike, who was once named Virginia Cattleman of the Year, developed his community-sensitive philosophy after working as a Peace Corps volunteer teaching math and physics in Tanzania and Uganda in the late 1960s, where he was one of a handful of Caucasians. He's learned that "whenever you're from outside the community—if you're more educated, if you're different—you have to display *more* sensitivity, to not only not offend, but to let people know you respect their way of life. There's going to be an assumption by people that you don't respect their way of life," he says, "so even if you do, the burden is on you to demonstrate your respect."

There's no better tool than listening to demonstrate that respect. Although you shouldn't be a stone-faced enigma when conversing with folks in the country, you do want to practice verbal self-restraint. Take your cue from the anatomical reality that you're equipped with two ears but only one mouth; try to use them in that proportion. In conversation you'll want to divulge some information about yourself to show that you're present, to reflect your personality and aspirations, but never talk beyond the point of audience interest. Think of listening as paying your dues.

As a newcomer, try to be the worker rather than the queen bee. Offer to grill hamburgers at the park benefit or pick up roadside trash for the Ruritans or Kiwanis Club. Helping out will give you a great observation booth from which to observe the community and discern areas where you can make a contribution. Listen to the music of the place, the way people talk. Listen to stories for what they reveal about people and the local culture. Resist the temptation to move in and become chairman of the board your first year in town. In fact, if at all possible, wait a few years before taking on significant leadership positions.

A few years back, a Sun Valley, Idaho area economic development director spoke out against a "new breed" of outsiders coming to town, getting elected to city council or appointed to boards, and becoming "a problem." Often they have "different values and their own agenda" and sometimes, she warned, they "take over." She referenced a pitched battle between newcomers who opposed the community's desire to appropriate funds to purchase porta-johns and picnic tables for hikers and mountain bikers. The newcomers, she said, "don't want public money spent to encourage summer tourism, even though it's a major source of income for many old-timers in our community."

Marion Goldwasser, who holds a master's degree in English and education from Stanford University, taught in the Carroll County school system for more than two decades. Together with her husband, Mike, she had to work to discard some of her urban habits, such as being "the first voice to speak out at a meeting." In Carroll County, she said, "people are more reticent; they take time to mull things over." What's more, people weigh their words carefully so as not to "burn bridges or have their words come back to haunt them."

Not only do you need to watch what you say, but you need to be careful how you put it. You do this because everyone's related by blood, friendship or business—you're liable to put your foot in your mouth if you utter a disparaging word about the car dealer with whom you just spoke (who turns out to be somebody's uncle, cousin or friend). Even if they don't know the person in question, remember that your attitude will be gauged by members of your new community. If you criticize a local, your listener may well conclude that he or she will be next on your verbal chopping block.

Hold this image in your mind before venting: Imagine that you're on the stand in a court of law and every word you utter is being taken into court record. This can be the case with country folks when drawing their first impression of a newcomer. Remember that the shelf life of your words is longer—by a factor of years—in the country than the city.

Every rural community is a world unto itself, and the "true believers"— the ones whose commitment to the community is absolute—are convinced that their town is the center of the universe. Some may call this provincialism, but we would argue that it's rather a healthy form of community spirit. In fact, you'll know you've "arrived" in your community when you reach for the *Madison Eagle* before *The Washington Post,* and when you become an unabashed community booster.

What's at the end of your gravel road may be your first genuine community, the first time in your life you've actually had a place to call your own. Unbeknownst to those who've never experienced it, smoothly-functioning community life offers an enormous source of sustenance: the pleasures of place and the fulfillment of our universal need for caring, continuity and belonging.

But don't expect to take to rural life like a duck to water—it takes time. You'll make tangible progress when you begin to crack the code of your new country community, build a network of relationships and a bedrock of trust, and finally convince people that you're no fly-by-nighter.

You'll know you've arrived when people stop asking you if you intend to stay.

Once this shift occurs and you've been welcomed into the community, you'll be amazed to find a neighbor at your doorstep offering advice, another neighbor gifting you with homegrown squash and, perhaps even selling you a ticket to the pancake benefit. (When you buy a ticket or two—even if you don't like pancakes—you know you've *really* arrived!)

Here are seven boiled-down tips for creating community in the country:

SLOW YOUR PACE.

The person in a hurry is viewed with wariness, even suspicion, in the country. You've moved out here to smell the roses, so breathe them in.

BE PUNCTUAL.

Leave yourself a cushion of time in the country. Rural Americans won't be impressed that you're "crazy busy"—too busy to be on time.

LET YOUR INDIVIDUALITY EMERGE...GRADUALLY.

Don't spring your differences on your new community. Take baby steps.

PITCH IN.

Country folks develop webs of favors and dependencies. You can work your way into these webs by spinning some threads of your own. Identify the need and then turn some old-fashioned good deeds.

JOIN CLUBS, CIVIC ORGANIZATIONS OR FAITH COMMUNITIES.

But if you do so, don't just put your name on the membership roll—take the organization seriously. Attend faithfully, help out and promote the group.

ALWAYS DONATE THINGS.

When asked, contribute what you can. If you can't make the full donation, do something. If you're asked to give $250 and it's not in your budget, give $25 and some encouraging words.

BUY LOCALLY.

Nothing engenders goodwill as quickly as patronizing local merchants—even if you have to pay a little extra. Buying locally helps build community.

FULL CIRCLE

So, once again, welcome.

Remember that fictional country porch, where we started this journey together? Remember that fictional farmer? Well, that fictional farmer — that was us. The folks who generated the ideas and enthusiasm and financial support necessary to bring this book to you. There are a lot of us — quite a crowd; at the back of the book we'll let you know just who we all are.

Well, a lot's happened since that encounter on the porch. We've traveled down a lot of winding backroads together. We've seen what it's like — both to be a farmer these days, and to be that farmer's neighbor. We've broken bread together a few times — we in the writing of this book, as we pictured you in our minds, and you as you read these pages. We've eaten some good meals together, and thanked the farmers who put our food on the table.

Now imagine you're back on that porch again. Again, the sun's going down, and you're watching it — with us. We hope you've enjoyed our company, and will continue to enjoy it. We know we've enjoyed yours.

So just remember this — you, who once we might have called a stranger. You're our friend now. And we certainly hope that we are yours. We're just tickled you've chosen to live here. We think it really is "God's country," living out here, where the pitcher of beauty just never runs dry — and we suspect you feel the same way.

There goes the sun. Turning fire engine red as it touches down on that purple ridge. Funny how it gets so big when it touches earth.

Funny, too, how strangers become good friends, sharing a place they love.

Welcome to the country! You've come home.

ABOUT THE AUTHOR

Frank Levering is a multi-dimensional talent – a farmer, author, playwright, poet, producer and scriptwriter, with a wide range of credits. He is the co-author with Wanda Urbanska of five books, including the critically acclaimed *Simple Living: One Couple's Search for a Better Life* (Viking/Penguin: 1992), *Moving to a Small Town: a Guidebook for Moving from Urban to Rural America* (Simon & Schuster: 1996), and *Nothing's Too Small to Make a Difference* (John F. Blair: 2004). He also has published a collection of poetry, *Blue Light* (Orchard Gap Press: 1997). Frank is the writer, director and co-producer of the PBS series, *Simple Living With Wanda Urbanska,* and his many plays—including the North Carolina state award-winning *It's Your Life*—have been performed in theatres around the country. In 1999, Frank founded and remains producer for the innovative environmental Cherry Orchard Theatre in Virginia.

Frank Levering was born in Mount Airy, North Carolina, and graduated from Wesleyan University in Connecticut, where he played football, studied with poet laureate Richard Wilbur, and earned a degree in English and American Studies. After graduating from Harvard Divinity School with a Master's in Theological Studies, Frank worked in Los Angeles as a screenwriter and freelance journalist for the *Los Angeles Herald-Examiner*. While in California, Frank co-wrote the film *Parasite 3D*, which was seen worldwide and was one of the top-grossing films of 1982. This campy, cult horror film introduced to the screen a then-teenage actress named Demi Moore. Frank is a recipient of the Governor's Screenwriting Award of Virginia.

The youngest of six in a Quaker family, Frank was raised on the family farm, Levering Orchard, just above the North Carolina state line in southern Virginia. In 1986, he and Wanda Urbanska moved from Los Angeles to the orchard, which is known throughout the Southeast for its pick-your-own cherries. Levering Orchard, which was founded by Frank's grandparents in 1908, is now the largest cherry orchard in the South.

Welcome to the Country

was brought to you by

THE BALLYSHANNON FUND

of the

CHARLOTTESVILLE AREA COMMUNITY FOUNDATION

Located in Charlottesville, Virginia,
near Mr. Jefferson's University of Virginia *("GO! 'Hoos!")*

Please visit

www.BallyshannonFund.com

where you will find links to a number of websites about agriculture,
livestock, forestry, wildlife, environmental issues, house-location,
construction methods, and more.

We welcome your suggestions for additional links we might add.
Please e-mail them to *info@ballyshannonfund.com*

The Ballyshannon Fund expresses its deep appreciation for hours of
assistance in interviewing newcomers to our community, talking to residents
of our area, for important research, and general good cheer from

SPENCER NEALE

of **The Virginia Farm Bureau Federation**

and

MARTHA A. WALKER

of **Virginia Cooperative Extension**

providing a connection to researched-based educational resources
from Virginia State University and Virginia Tech *("GO! Hokies!")*

(It's all about family, here, except during football season.)

Finally, we are very grateful to our author

FRANK LEVERING

Frank grew up in southern Virginia on his family's cherry orchard.
The Levering family still runs it today, 100 years after it was originally planted.